SEO GOD

Hayden Van Der Post

Reactive Publishing

CONTENTS

PREFACE

Welcome to SEO God: A Comprehensive Guide to SEO for 2025—a book born from the passion to help you conquer the digital realm and transform your online presence into a force to be reckoned with. As you hold this book in your hands, imagine a future where your brand isn't just another name on the internet, but an authority that shapes trends, drives organic traffic, and converts curious clicks into loyal customers.

The digital landscape is evolving at breakneck speed. Gone are the days when simple keyword stuffing and basic link-building tactics reigned supreme. Today's SEO is a sophisticated dance between technology and human behavior—a dynamic interplay of algorithms, artificial intelligence, and creative storytelling. Within these pages, you will discover a roadmap designed to navigate this ever-changing environment, providing you with the tools and insights to emerge as an SEO powerhouse in 2025 and beyond.

This guide is not just another manual; it's a blueprint for transforming your digital strategy. In Chapter 1, we set the stage by diving deep into the evolution of search engines and the seismic shifts in user behavior. You'll come to understand why SEO is more critical than ever in today's digital age, and how its rise is directly tied to the success of every ambitious business.

As you journey through the next chapters, you'll unravel

mysteries such as how search engines really work—demystifying the core principles of crawling, indexing, and ranking. You will explore innovative topics ranging from the inner workings of artificial intelligence in search algorithms to the emerging influence of voice and visual search. Learn to harness the power of keyword research in a new era, craft compelling content that resonates with your audience, and ensure your website's technical architecture is built like a fortress.

But what truly sets this book apart is its forward-thinking approach. We don't just cover the tactics that work today; we peer into the future of SEO. Imagine harnessing the potential of blockchain technology, leveraging augmented reality to create immersive digital experiences, and preparing your website for the next major algorithm update before your competitors even know what hit them. Through chapters dedicated to on-page optimization, technical mastery, content creation, backlinks, local SEO, and e-commerce challenges, you are equipped with an arsenal of strategies to dominate search results in a competitive marketplace.

Every section of SEO God is crafted with one purpose in mind—to empower you to become the authority in your niche. Whether you're a digital marketer striving for breakthrough results, an entrepreneur determined to build a formidable online brand, or a seasoned SEO specialist looking to stay ahead of the curve, this comprehensive guide is your companion on the journey to digital mastery.

Unleashing the power of SEO isn't just about technical know-how; it's about embracing change and using innovation to connect with your audience on a deeper level. It's about understanding that every keyword, every link, every line of code, and every piece of content is a building block in the grand structure of your digital empire.

Prepare to embark on a transformative journey. As you progress through the chapters, you'll not only be learning essential strategies but also igniting the spark that will set your online endeavors ablaze. This is your time to step into the light, to become the SEO God of your own digital destiny, and to witness the incredible impact that a well-executed SEO strategy can have on your business and your life.

Welcome to the future of search—and welcome to your new reality. Let's get started.

CHAPTER 1: INTRODUCTION TO SEO IN 2025

Evolution of Search Engines

Search engines have undergone remarkable transformations since their inception, evolving from simple directories into sophisticated systems that can comprehend human intent and deliver highly relevant results. Early search engines like Archie and AltaVista served as basic tools that indexed web pages based solely on keyword matches. Users would enter their queries, and the search engine would return a list of sites containing those exact terms. While this functionality was groundbreaking at the time, it often lacked the depth and nuance needed to satisfy users fully, resulting in less-than-ideal experiences.

The introduction of Google in the late 1990s marked a dramatic shift in this landscape. With its innovative PageRank algorithm, Google analyzed the relationships between web pages, considering not only keyword frequency but also the quality and quantity of links pointing to each page. This approach created a more refined ranking system that rewarded content deemed valuable by other sites. As users became accustomed to receiving more relevant search results, their expectations for accuracy increased significantly.

The early 2000s saw an explosion of new features aimed at enhancing user experience. Local search capabilities emerged, allowing users to find businesses and services tailored to their geographical area. This development acknowledged that many search queries were tied to immediate needs—whether locating a nearby restaurant or sourcing local services. As mobile devices gained popularity, search engines adapted even further, optimizing for mobile queries and emphasizing location-based results.

In recent years, artificial intelligence (AI) has taken center stage in the evolution of search engines. Algorithms like RankBrain have integrated machine learning capabilities, enabling systems to grasp context and semantics more effectively than ever before. For example, when a user searches for "best Italian restaurant," the engine can infer related preferences based on past behavior or regional trends, eliminating the need for exact keyword matches. This advancement marks a significant leap toward conversational search experiences where users can interact with technology in a more natural way.

Voice search has also reshaped our approach to queries. Users increasingly ask questions verbally rather than typing keywords —this shift requires different optimization strategies for SEO professionals. Take this example, someone might ask, "What's the best pizza place near me?" In this scenario, long-tail keywords become crucial as they reflect natural speech patterns rather than traditional keyword optimization practices.

Visual search capabilities are also making waves, with tools like Google Lens enabling users to conduct searches using images instead of words. Imagine taking a photo of an unfamiliar flower; instead of describing it in text, you simply upload the image for instant identification and information retrieval. This evolution challenges marketers to think creatively about how they present visual content online, ensuring it is optimized not only for textual searches but also for visual recognition systems.

These developments culminate in an era where user experience is paramount—today's search engines prioritize delivering personalized results through an ever-deepening understanding of individual preferences and behaviors. Businesses must now focus not only on traditional SEO techniques but also embrace innovative approaches that leverage AI-driven insights into user intent and engagement metrics.

As we delve deeper into these advancements in our exploration of SEO strategies tailored for 2025 and beyond, it becomes clear that staying ahead requires us to embrace change while continually refining our understanding of what drives user satisfaction in this rapidly evolving digital landscape.

The Importance of SEO in Today's Digital Age

The digital landscape has undergone significant transformation, highlighting the essential role of SEO in achieving online visibility and success. With billions of searches conducted daily, it's crucial for businesses to grasp how search engines prioritize content in order to connect effectively with their target audience. SEO has evolved from a supplementary marketing tactic into a fundamental component of any successful online strategy.

In today's interconnected world, user behavior plays a pivotal role in shaping expectations. People seek immediate answers that are tailored to their specific needs. When they enter a query or use voice commands, they expect results that not only align with their keywords but also resonate with their intent. This expectation places pressure on brands to optimize their content effectively, ensuring it stands out in an increasingly crowded marketplace.

In this environment, effective SEO serves as a vital link between potential customers and the solutions that businesses offer.

Websites that rank highly in search results attract more organic traffic, leading to greater opportunities for conversion. The statistics reinforce this point: nearly 60% of clicks on search engine results pages (SERPs) go to the top three listings. This emphasizes the critical nature of SEO; falling to lower rankings means reduced visibility and lost revenue potential.

Also, the surge in mobile browsing has intensified the need for SEO strategies tailored to user habits. With over half of all web traffic originating from mobile devices, search engines have adjusted their algorithms accordingly. Google's mobile-first indexing highlights that a website's performance on mobile significantly influences its ranking in search results. Brands must ensure that their websites load quickly on mobile devices and provide a seamless user experience, which includes optimizing navigation and making content easily accessible without excessive scrolling or clicking.

An important part of modern SEO is leveraging data analytics. Tools like Google Analytics and Search Console provide invaluable insights into user behavior, empowering marketers to make informed decisions about their strategies. Take this example, examining which keywords drive traffic or identifying pages with high bounce rates can guide adjustments that enhance user engagement and retention.

As businesses increasingly depend on digital channels for growth, the significance of local SEO becomes even more pronounced. Consumers frequently search for products and services nearby, making it essential for brands to optimize for local searches effectively. Claiming and refining Google My Business listings can substantially improve visibility in local search results. This involves providing accurate business information, crafting engaging descriptions, and promptly responding to customer reviews—all crucial elements for enhancing local presence.

The interplay between social media and SEO strategies is also noteworthy today. While social signals may not directly affect rankings, social media platforms act as powerful distribution channels that can amplify content reach and engagement. A robust social media presence drives traffic back to websites while fostering community interaction around brands.

Looking ahead, the integration of AI in search algorithms will continue to shape the future of SEO. Understanding AI-driven changes will enable marketers to adapt proactively, embracing innovations such as voice search optimization and machine learning applications. This proactive approach can give brands a competitive edge over those who may struggle to keep up.

Navigating this complex landscape requires more than just adherence to best practices; it necessitates a forward-thinking mindset focused on continuous learning and adaptation. As trends evolve at an unprecedented pace, those who excel at leveraging SEO as an integral part of their marketing strategy will thrive in an increasingly competitive digital arena.

SEO is no longer solely about driving traffic; it's about understanding people—their desires, habits, and pain points —and delivering value through relevant content experiences tailored specifically for them. By prioritizing these elements within your digital strategy today, you lay the foundation for sustained growth tomorrow in this fast-evolving realm where every click counts.

Key SEO Concepts and Terminology

Navigating the intricate landscape of digital marketing requires a solid grasp of key SEO concepts and terminology. As search engine optimization continually evolves, understanding foundational terms becomes crucial for making informed decisions. This lexicon forms the backbone of effective strategies, empowering marketers to communicate ideas clearly and execute tactics with precision.

Essentially of SEO is the concept of keywords—phrases or terms that users input into search engines while searching for information. Selecting the right keywords goes beyond simply targeting high-traffic phrases; it necessitates an understanding of user intent—the specific needs or questions driving a search. For example, a person searching for "best running shoes" may be at a different stage in their buying journey compared to someone looking for "running shoe reviews." Recognizing these distinctions enables marketers to create content that aligns with diverse user intents.

Transitioning from keywords, we delve into on-page SEO, which encompasses all elements directly controllable on a website aimed at improving visibility. This includes optimizing title tags, header tags (H1, H2, etc.), and meta descriptions, all of which signal to search engines what a page is about while enhancing click-through rates from search engine results pages (SERPs). A compelling title tag, such as "Top 10 Running Shoes for Beginners – Comfort Meets Performance," effectively conveys value while incorporating relevant keywords.

Beyond individual sites lies off-page SEO, which focuses on external factors that impact rankings. Here, backlinks—the links from other websites pointing to yours—play a pivotal role. They act as endorsements; the more quality backlinks your site garners, the more authoritative it appears to search engines. A practical approach involves reaching out to industry influencers or bloggers who might share your content or link back to it in their articles.

Technical SEO takes us behind the scenes to explore elements that affect how well search engines crawl and index a site's pages. Factors such as site speed, mobile-friendliness, and secure connections (HTTPS) are critical here. Take this example, Google's algorithm prioritizes fast-loading pages for their positive impact on user experience; tools like Google PageSpeed Insights can identify areas needing improvement.

In today's SEO landscape, understanding user engagement metrics is equally important. Metrics like bounce rate—how quickly users leave a page after viewing it—and dwell time—the time spent on a page before returning to SERPs—offer valuable insights into content effectiveness. A high bounce rate may indicate that the content does not meet user expectations.

The rise of voice search adds further complexity to keyword strategy and content creation. As people increasingly use voice-activated devices like Amazon Echo or Google Home, optimizing for natural language queries becomes essential. Take this example, phrasing such as "What are the best running shoes?" diverges from traditional keyword targeting yet reflects how users communicate naturally.

Simultaneously, local SEO has gained significance due to the growing reliance on local searches for products and services. Consistency in NAP (Name, Address, Phone Number) across platforms ensures businesses appear correctly in local results; discrepancies can confuse both users and search engines alike.

Additionally, understanding schema markup enhances visibility by enabling richer search results through structured data. Implementing schema helps search engines comprehend your content's context—be it an article, recipe, or product—and display this information directly in SERPs.

Lastly, E-A-T—Expertise, Authoritativeness, Trustworthiness—is an emerging term gaining traction in SEO discussions. Search engines increasingly prioritize websites that demonstrate these qualities through high-quality content creation and credible sources backing claims made within articles.

As you immerse yourself in these essential concepts and terminology surrounding SEO, remember that they interconnect and influence every aspect of today's digital marketing strategies. Mastering them not only enhances communication within your team but also equips you to adapt swiftly as trends evolve—a vital skill for achieving sustained success in this dynamic field where understanding underpins actionable strategy.

Changes in User Behavior and Search Trends

To craft an effective SEO strategy in 2025, it is essential to understand the evolving patterns of user behavior and search trends. As technology advances, so too do the ways in which users engage with search engines, making it imperative for marketers to adapt swiftly. A significant factor in this evolution is the increasing reliance on mobile devices, which has dramatically reshaped the online landscape. Recent studies show that mobile searches now account for over half of all online traffic, underscoring the necessity of optimizing websites for a seamless mobile experience rather than treating it as a mere enhancement.

User behavior encompasses more than just keyword searches; it also includes how individuals interact with content once they find it. One notable trend is the growing preference for long-form content. Users are increasingly drawn to comprehensive articles that provide thorough answers to their questions. This shift highlights the importance of producing quality content that not only targets specific keywords but also aligns closely with user intent. Take this example, an article on "best running shoes" could benefit from detailed reviews, comparisons, and links to purchase options, effectively addressing users' needs at various stages of their decision-making process.

Personalization has also transformed how search results are tailored to users. Search engines now leverage data from past behaviors to deliver customized results based on individual preferences. This trend emphasizes the need for marketers to gain a deep understanding of their target audience. Utilizing tools like Google Analytics can provide valuable insights into user demographics and behavioral patterns—information that can inform content creation and SEO strategies. For example, if analytics indicate a strong interest in eco-friendly products among your audience, developing targeted content around sustainable running gear could lead to higher engagement.

Another significant factor influencing user interactions with search engines is the rise of voice search. With voice-activated assistants such as Siri and Google Assistant becoming commonplace, there is a noticeable shift toward more conversational keyword phrases. Rather than focusing solely on short-tail keywords like "running shoes," marketers should consider longer queries such as "Which running shoes are best for flat feet?" By optimizing for natural language queries, businesses can maintain relevance as voice search becomes an integral part of daily life.

Local SEO has also undergone significant changes due to shifts in consumer behavior. The demand for local information has surged, particularly among mobile users seeking immediate solutions—such as nearby restaurants or stores. Claiming and optimizing Google My Business listings can enhance visibility in local searches, allowing businesses to appear prominently when potential customers look for services nearby.

The influence of user-generated content cannot be overlooked either. Today's consumers tend to trust peer reviews and feedback more than traditional advertising methods. Platforms like Yelp and TripAdvisor facilitate the sharing of experiences and can significantly impact others' decisions. Encouraging satisfied customers to leave positive reviews can bolster your site's credibility and authority—both crucial elements in local SEO and overall rankings.

As engagement metrics increasingly dictate content performance within search engine results pages (SERPs), understanding these indicators becomes essential. Bounce rates reveal whether users find what they're looking for upon landing on your page; high bounce rates may indicate a disconnect between user intent and the provided content. Conversely, metrics like dwell time—how long visitors stay on a page before returning to search results—can signal successful engagement with quality content.

Emerging technologies such as augmented reality (AR) present new opportunities for enhancing user experiences. Brands that incorporate AR features into their websites allow customers to visualize products in real-time—whether trying on clothes virtually or seeing how furniture fits within their living spaces before making purchases.

Lastly, data privacy concerns have dramatically shifted user behavior in recent years. With increased scrutiny surrounding data collection practices, consumers are becoming more cautious about sharing personal information online. Marketers must navigate these challenges by being transparent about data usage while still providing personalized experiences without compromising privacy.

In summary, adapting to changes in user behavior requires an ongoing commitment to innovation in your SEO practices. By examining these evolving trends—from mobile optimization and personalization to local searches and voice queries— you'll see how each element interconnects within the broader landscape of digital marketing strategies. Embracing these shifts not only positions your brand favorably in SERPs but also fosters deeper connections with users by genuinely addressing their needs and expectations throughout their online journeys.

Overview of Major Updates in SEO

Recent updates in SEO have become essential, reshaping how businesses formulate their digital marketing strategies. In recent years, search engines like Google have introduced significant algorithm changes that directly influence ranking factors. For anyone aiming to maintain or enhance their online visibility, understanding these updates is crucial.

One of the most notable shifts has been the increased focus on quality content and user experience. Google's introduction of the E-A-T principle—Expertise, Authoritativeness, and Trustworthiness—has transformed the evaluation of content. Websites that exhibit a high level of expertise in their respective fields often achieve better rankings, especially in sensitive sectors like health and finance. For example, a site providing medical advice must not only present accurate information but also establish credibility through author qualifications and references from reputable sources.

Another important development is the Core Web Vitals update, which introduced specific metrics aimed at improving page loading performance, interactivity, and visual stability. Websites that do not meet these standards risk falling in rankings. To enhance site performance, businesses can utilize tools like Google PageSpeed Insights to identify issues such as slow loading times or inadequate mobile responsiveness. If your website takes longer than three seconds to load on mobile devices, optimizing images or leveraging browser caching can be effective strategies to boost speed.

The rise of voice search optimization is also noteworthy, driven by the increasing use of smart speakers and voice-activated devices. As users gravitate towards conversational queries, it's essential to optimize for natural language. This involves anticipating questions users may ask aloud rather than relying solely on traditional keyword phrases. For example, instead of focusing on "best sneakers," you might optimize for "What are the best sneakers for running?" Tailoring content to fit these longer phrases can significantly improve your visibility in voice search results.

Also, Google's emphasis on local SEO has grown, particularly with updates highlighting the importance of relevance in localized searches. Businesses should ensure their listings are accurate across various platforms while actively encouraging customer reviews. Utilizing tools like Google My Business not only enhances visibility but also fosters engagement with potential customers seeking nearby services.

Mobile-first indexing reinforces the need for responsive web design more than ever. With a majority of searches now conducted on mobile devices, having a mobile-friendly site is critical for maintaining rankings and attracting traffic. Websites must prioritize designs that seamlessly adapt across devices while providing easy navigation and accessibility.

The influence of artificial intelligence (AI) on SEO strategies is also significant. AI-driven algorithms are increasingly capable of understanding user intent and context more effectively. Businesses leveraging AI tools to analyze search patterns can gain valuable insights into consumer behavior, allowing for more precise adjustments to their content strategies.

Additionally, algorithm updates often coincide with a heightened focus on data privacy. As consumers become increasingly aware of how their data is used online, businesses must prioritize transparency regarding their data practices while still delivering personalized experiences based on user behavior without infringing on privacy concerns.

Real-world examples illustrate how adapting to these major updates can lead to notable improvements in organic traffic and conversions. Companies like Moz have reported substantial increases in rankings after aligning their content strategies with E-A-T principles following major updates.

As you navigate this ever-changing landscape of SEO updates, staying informed about changes allows for quick pivots when necessary while continuously optimizing your website's performance and relevance in a dynamic digital world. Embracing these updates goes beyond mere compliance; it's about enhancing user experience and building lasting relationships with your audience through trust and quality interactions online. Each update serves as a reminder that agility is essential—staying ahead requires vigilance and a commitment to ongoing learning and adaptation within your SEO practices.

The Future of Organic Search

The future of organic search is increasingly influenced by the convergence of technology, user behavior, and evolving search engine algorithms. For businesses to thrive in this dynamic landscape, they must be ready to adapt their strategies and embrace innovation at every opportunity. An important part of this transformation lies in understanding how advancements in artificial intelligence (AI) and machine learning will reshape the way search engines interpret and respond to user queries.

As AI technologies continue to advance, they empower search engines to analyze vast amounts of data with remarkable speed and accuracy. This evolution necessitates a shift in SEO strategies from a narrow focus on keyword density and backlinks toward a deeper understanding of context and user intent. For example, Google's RankBrain leverages machine learning to decipher ambiguous queries, providing results that reflect not just the keywords but also the underlying meaning behind them. That's why, content creators must think beyond traditional SEO tactics and develop content that specifically addresses the questions or problems users encounter.

In addition, the rise of conversational interfaces and voice search is transforming how people engage with search engines. Users now expect answers presented in a more natural, dialogue-like format. This shift means that optimizing content for voice queries requires anticipating longer phrases or complete questions rather than relying solely on single keywords. Take this example, instead of optimizing for "pizza near me," an effective strategy would involve crafting responses that directly address inquiries like "What are the best pizza places nearby?" By incorporating conversational language into your content, you not only enhance visibility in voice searches but also align with user expectations for prompt and relevant answers.

Local SEO is also poised for continued growth as mobile usage drives local searches. The integration of AI into location-based services enables search engines to deliver hyper-localized results tailored to users' immediate environments. Businesses can capitalize on this trend by ensuring their local listings are accurate across platforms like Google My Business and actively engaging with customer reviews. Encouraging satisfied customers to leave positive feedback can significantly improve visibility in local searches.

User experience (UX) will play an increasingly critical role in the future landscape of organic search. Google's algorithm updates are placing greater emphasis on websites that provide seamless experiences across devices. A fast-loading website that is easy to navigate and offers valuable content will be essential for retaining visitors and improving rankings. Google's Core Web Vitals metrics serve as vital benchmarks; sites that optimize for these criteria can expect favorable treatment from search algorithms.

While content quality remains paramount, adapting it to future trends is essential. As audiences become more discerning, they seek depth over superficiality—content must resonate emotionally and deliver genuine value to stand out amidst the noise. Take this example, brands that incorporate storytelling into their content can forge lasting connections with their audience, enhancing both engagement and shareability.

Emerging technologies like augmented reality (AR) may also impact organic search dynamics by providing immersive experiences that blend seamlessly with traditional search results. Imagine a scenario where users can virtually try products before making a purchase—all driven by organic search results tailored to their preferences. This potential shift highlights the importance of remaining agile and forward-thinking in your SEO strategies.

Privacy concerns are set to shape the future landscape as well; consumers are increasingly vigilant about how their data is utilized online. In response, businesses must find a balance between personalization—using data insights for tailored experiences—and transparency regarding data practices. A commitment to ethical handling of user data not only fosters trust but can significantly enhance brand reputation.

As you navigate this evolving terrain, agility is key—staying informed about technological advancements allows you to swiftly adapt your SEO strategies when necessary. Embrace innovation while maintaining a clear focus on user experience and quality content creation; these elements will be crucial as you position your brand at the forefront of organic search success.

the future isn't just about keeping pace; it's about leading change through creative strategies grounded in technology and human-centric design principles. By effectively harnessing AI tools and prioritizing authentic engagement with users, you'll differentiate yourself in an increasingly competitive digital marketplace where adaptability defines success.

Objectives of This Book

The objectives of this book are to equip you with the knowledge and skills necessary to navigate the rapidly evolving world of SEO as we approach 2025. More than just a technical manual, it serves as a comprehensive roadmap designed to enhance your understanding and application of SEO strategies tailored to today's digital landscape.

We begin by demystifying the complex mechanics of search engines. By breaking down key processes such as crawling, indexing, and ranking, you'll gain a clearer perspective on how these elements interconnect. This foundational knowledge will empower you to craft SEO strategies that are both effective and resilient in the face of ever-changing search algorithms.

Next, we'll explore the practical applications of keyword research. This book provides advanced tools and techniques that extend beyond traditional keyword strategies. You'll learn how to analyze user intent and segment keywords into actionable insights. Through real-world examples, we'll examine how various industries utilize keyword research to drive targeted traffic, improve conversion rates, and ultimately enhance their bottom lines.

On-page optimization will also be thoroughly covered, focusing on the elements that directly influence search rankings. We'll dissect components such as title tags, meta descriptions, header tags, and image optimization. With concrete walkthroughs illustrating these concepts in action, you'll feel confident implementing changes that transform your pages into effective gateways for attracting organic traffic.

As we move beyond on-page tactics, technical SEO will take center stage. With search engines growing increasingly sophisticated, maintaining a well-structured website is essential. You'll learn about XML sitemaps, robots.txt files, and canonicalization techniques—each critical for ensuring that search engines can efficiently crawl your site without encountering obstacles.

The integration of AI and machine learning into SEO practices is another significant focus of this book. By understanding how these technologies influence user behavior and search algorithms, you can harness them to create personalized experiences for users. This guide offers insights into tools that utilize AI for content optimization and audience targeting— setting the stage for innovative approaches in your campaigns.

Essentially of any successful SEO strategy lies content creation. Here, we aim to develop your ability to produce high-quality content that resonates with your audience while adhering to SEO best practices. You will learn how to strike a balance between creativity and technical requirements, ensuring your content not only ranks well but also engages readers meaningfully.

In our examination of local SEO tactics, you'll discover how businesses can dominate their local markets through effective optimization strategies. As mobile technology advances and local searches become increasingly prevalent, mastering Google

My Business listings and managing customer reviews becomes crucial for driving foot traffic and enhancing visibility.

Measuring success is vital in any endeavor; thus, this book emphasizes the role of analytics in evaluating your SEO performance. You'll become adept at interpreting data from Google Analytics and Search Console, gaining actionable insights that inform future strategies. We will also introduce custom dashboards as a means to streamline reporting processes and effectively track key performance indicators.

As you progress through each section, consider how these concepts interrelate; they work together to form a cohesive SEO strategy rather than functioning in isolation. The knowledge you gain here is not merely theoretical—it provides actionable guidance designed to transform your approach to digital marketing.

Through practical exercises and case studies reflecting real-world applications of SEO strategies across diverse industries, you'll be challenged to think critically about how each aspect impacts overall performance. Embrace this opportunity for growth; it's crafted not only to inform but also to inspire innovative solutions tailored specifically to your business objectives.

our goal is clear: by mastering the intricacies presented within these pages, you will position yourself as a leader in the field of SEO—capable of navigating complexity while delivering tangible results in an ever-changing digital ecosystem. Prepare yourself to engage deeply with each topic and emerge empowered as an adept practitioner ready for the challenges ahead.

CHAPTER 2:
UNDERSTANDING
SEARCH ENGINES

How Search Engines Work

Search engines are intricate systems designed to connect users with information, employing sophisticated processes to deliver relevant results almost instantaneously. Essentially of these operations are three essential functions: crawling, indexing, and ranking. A clear understanding of how these components interact is fundamental for developing effective SEO strategies.

The process begins with crawling. Search engines deploy bots—often called crawlers or spiders—to discover new and updated content across the internet. These crawlers navigate websites by following links, similar to how a person would browse through pages. To enhance the efficiency of this crawling process, it's important to maintain a logical site structure. For example, using an XML sitemap can significantly help crawlers find all the relevant pages on your site without getting lost in complex navigation.

After content is discovered through crawling, it must be

indexed before it can appear in search results. Indexing involves analyzing and storing information from web pages in a massive database. During this phase, search engines evaluate various factors such as keywords, content quality, and user engagement metrics. If a page isn't indexed properly due to technical issues or subpar content quality, it will remain invisible to searchers. Regularly checking your website's index status with tools like Google Search Console is crucial for ensuring that all valuable pages are included in the index.

Once indexing is complete, ranking comes into play. This is where the complexities of search algorithms are most evident. After indexing, search engines assess which pages are most relevant to a user's query based on numerous criteria, including keyword relevance, site authority, user engagement metrics (like click-through rates), loading speed, and mobile-friendliness. Sophisticated algorithms work to provide users with the best possible answers quickly. Take this example, if two websites offer similar information about "best coffee brewers," the one with greater authority and superior user experience is likely to rank higher.

To illustrate how these components work together, consider a blog post about "best hiking trails." If you create an engaging post but overlook SEO fundamentals—such as proper metadata or optimized images—it may never be crawled or indexed effectively. Conversely, even if you meticulously optimize your content but have poor website architecture that leads to crawl errors, your site could still be invisible to potential visitors.

Artificial Intelligence (AI) has added another layer of sophistication to how search engines operate today. With machine learning algorithms analyzing vast amounts of data on user interactions and preferences, search engines can personalize results more effectively than ever before. For example, Google's RankBrain uses AI to better understand queries by considering context rather than relying solely on keywords.

And, user behavior increasingly influences search outcomes as AI adapts based on feedback gathered from millions of searches each day. A well-designed SEO strategy must account for this evolving landscape; understanding how users interact with search results—beyond just the keywords they use—is crucial.

The rise of voice search presents yet another aspect that affects how search engines function today. People often phrase their voice queries differently than typed ones; therefore, optimizing for conversational language becomes vital for ensuring visibility in voice searches. Take this example, focusing on questions like "What are the best vegan restaurants near me?" rather than simply targeting "vegan restaurants" can lead to increased traffic from voice-enabled devices.

These implications extend beyond keyword optimization; they require a holistic approach that includes improvements in site speed and mobile responsiveness—both of which will be essential for rankings in 2025 and beyond.

In this evolving landscape, discussions around semantic search capabilities implemented by major players like Google and Bing are also crucial. Semantic search enhances understanding by prioritizing meaning over mere keyword matching—a critical shift that reflects modern users' intent-driven inquiries.

By embracing these foundational principles, you will establish a robust framework not only for crafting effective SEO strategies but also for adapting them as technology continues to evolve through 2025 and beyond. The interplay between crawling technologies, indexing processes, and ranking mechanics creates an ecosystem where optimization efforts yield tangible results when executed strategically.

Recognizing that every element plays a role in this intricate web fosters deeper insights into improving visibility within an increasingly competitive digital environment. As new trends emerge from technological advancements or shifts in user behavior patterns, being responsive becomes vital.

Understanding these mechanisms is essential—not just for developing effective strategies but also for ensuring long-term adaptability amid rapid changes across the online landscape.

Crawling, Indexing, and Ranking

Search engines are complex systems designed to connect users with information, relying on three essential processes: crawling, indexing, and ranking. Each of these functions is vital for how content is discovered, stored, and presented to users. By understanding these processes, you can enhance your SEO efforts and effectively navigate the ever-evolving digital landscape.

Crawling is the initial step in this triad. During this phase, search engine bots—commonly known as crawlers or spiders—scan the web for new or updated content by following hyperlinks from one page to another. To facilitate efficient crawling, it's crucial to structure your website logically. Implementing an XML sitemap can significantly assist crawlers in locating all relevant pages without getting lost in a complicated navigation system. Think of your website's structure as a well-organized library: if books are categorized by genre and clearly labeled, visitors (or crawlers) can easily find what they need.

After content is crawled, it enters the indexing phase. Here, search engines analyze and catalog the information from each page into their vast databases. During indexing, factors such as content quality, keyword relevance, and user engagement metrics—like bounce rates—are taken into account. Pages that do not meet specific criteria due to poor optimization or technical issues may not be indexed at all, rendering them invisible in search results. Regularly checking your site's index status through tools like Google Search Console is essential to identify barriers that could prevent your valuable content from being included.

Once indexing is complete, the ranking process begins. This phase involves evaluating which pages best address user queries.

Search algorithms play a crucial role here, weighing numerous factors such as keyword relevance, site authority, engagement metrics (like click-through rates), loading speed, and mobile-friendliness to determine a page's rank in response to specific queries. For example, if two articles discuss "how to start a vegetable garden," the one with high-quality content supported by authoritative sources is more likely to rank higher than one that lacks depth and has slow loading times.

To illustrate how these processes work together, consider writing an article on "best running shoes." Even if you create an insightful post filled with valuable advice, neglecting key SEO elements like title tags or meta descriptions can hinder your search visibility. Conversely, a technically optimized article may still underperform if your website has crawl errors or poorly structured content.

The integration of artificial intelligence (AI) has further transformed how search engines operate today. Algorithms now utilize machine learning techniques to analyze extensive datasets related to user behavior and preferences. Take this example, Google's RankBrain enhances its understanding of queries by focusing on context rather than relying solely on keywords. If users frequently engage with results featuring "eco-friendly running shoes" after searching for "running shoes," algorithms will adapt accordingly over time.

User interactions are crucial in shaping search outcomes; search engines continuously adjust based on the feedback collected from countless searches each day. Developing an effective SEO strategy requires an understanding of this dynamic landscape: recognizing that user behavior extends beyond tracking keywords to interpreting engagement patterns and user intent.

Voice search has also emerged as a transformative element in how search engines function. Queries spoken aloud often differ significantly from those typed, making it imperative to optimize for conversational phrases to ensure visibility in voice searches.

Instead of targeting generic terms like "running shoes," focus on questions such as "What are the best running shoes for flat feet?" This shift not only captures voice search traffic but also aligns better with users' natural language patterns.

These trends demand more than just keyword optimization strategies; they call for a comprehensive approach that includes improvements in site speed and mobile responsiveness—critical factors for maintaining competitive rankings into 2025 and beyond.

With advancements like semantic search reshaping platforms such as Google and Bing, grasping this capability is vital. Semantic search prioritizes meaning over mere keyword matching, reflecting the intent-driven inquiries of contemporary users.

By integrating these foundational principles of crawling, indexing, and ranking into your SEO strategy, you will create a flexible framework capable of adapting alongside technological advancements through 2025 and beyond. Recognizing the importance of each component fosters deeper insights into enhancing your website's visibility in today's competitive digital marketplace.

Understanding these intricate mechanisms goes beyond refining strategies; it prepares you for long-term adaptability amidst the rapid changes shaping online interactions and user expectations globally. As new trends emerge—from AI innovations revolutionizing data handling to shifts in user preferences—the ability to respond effectively becomes crucial for any successful digital marketing endeavor.

The Role of Algorithms

Algorithms are the foundation of search engines, influencing how content is evaluated and ranked. Their complexity determines not only what shows up on the first page of search results but also how businesses shape their online strategies. For anyone serious about optimizing for SEO in 2025, understanding the role of algorithms is essential.

At their essence, algorithms consist of intricate rules and calculations that interpret user queries to deliver relevant results. Take this example, Google's algorithm employs hundreds of factors, ranging from keyword usage to user engagement metrics. However, it's not solely about matching keywords to search terms; it's about grasping context, relevance, and user intent. This evolution has been significant; long gone are the days when simple keyword stuffing could secure a top ranking. Today's algorithms prioritize content quality, authority, and even signals from user behavior.

Let's explore how specific updates have shaped algorithm behavior over time. A notable example is Google's BERT update, launched in late 2019. This update marked a pivotal shift toward natural language processing in search queries, allowing the algorithm to comprehend language nuances and better understand user intent. Take this example, when a user searches for "how to tie a tie," BERT enables Google to provide more tailored content, reducing the chances of returning irrelevant guides or videos.

Machine learning also plays a crucial role in algorithm development. It allows search engines to improve continuously by learning from past searches and outcomes. As users interact with search results—clicking on links or bouncing back—the algorithm gathers insights into what works and what doesn't. This feedback loop means that SEO strategies must be adaptable; practices effective today may lose their impact tomorrow as algorithms evolve.

Real-world applications highlight this adaptability. Take an e-commerce site that optimizes its product descriptions not just for keywords but for conversational queries like "best running shoes for flat feet." By aligning content with how potential buyers naturally phrase their questions—rather than relying solely on technical jargon—the site can better capture traffic from voice searches and nuanced queries.

And, this focus on user experience goes beyond keyword optimization. Metrics such as dwell time and click-through rates inform algorithms about how well content meets user needs. High-quality content encourages visitors to stay longer on pages and explore additional resources—behaviors that signal relevance and authority back to the algorithm.

Staying informed about algorithm changes can also provide businesses with a competitive advantage. Monitoring announcements from major search engines allows practitioners to anticipate shifts in ranking criteria or new features designed to enhance user experience. For example, Google's Core Web Vitals update highlighted the importance of page speed, responsiveness, and visual stability—elements that webmasters must prioritize now more than ever.

As we move toward 2025, embracing data-driven insights becomes increasingly important for SEO professionals. Analytics tools can help identify which aspects of a site resonate most with users while revealing opportunities for improvement based on algorithmic changes. A/B testing different strategies enables marketers to understand firsthand what aligns best with current algorithm preferences.

To wrap things up, algorithms act as both gatekeepers and facilitators in the digital landscape—shaping how users discover information while evolving based on user interactions and feedback. Mastery over these elements is crucial not only for achieving high rankings but also for delivering real value through content optimized for audience needs. The interplay between understanding algorithms and strategic content creation will define success in SEO as we approach 2025—an era where adaptability is not just beneficial but imperative.

Artificial Intelligence in Search

Artificial intelligence (AI) has evolved from a futuristic concept into a vital force reshaping the SEO landscape. As algorithms grow more sophisticated, integrating AI into search engine optimization strategies is no longer optional; it's essential. This interplay between AI and search engines extends beyond merely improving rankings; it's about understanding how user interactions can inform and transform digital content strategies.

One of the most significant impacts of AI on search is its capacity to analyze vast datasets swiftly and accurately. Take this example, Google's RankBrain employs machine learning to process search queries and discern their context, ultimately delivering more relevant results for users. It goes beyond simple keyword matching, considering factors like the nature of the query, user behavior, and even regional nuances. Take the example of a user searching for "best sushi near me." RankBrain assesses previous searches and interactions to provide results that cater not only to keyword relevance but also to local preferences, illustrating how AI enhances traditional keyword strategies.

Incorporating AI-driven tools can shift your SEO strategy from reactive to proactive. Tools like Clearscope and Surfer SEO leverage AI to analyze top-ranking content, offering insights on related keywords, readability scores, and structural elements that resonate with audiences. This empowers marketers to create content that not only targets specific keywords but also aligns with what engages users most effectively. If an analysis reveals that successful articles frequently use certain phrases or address specific questions, integrating these insights can significantly boost your content's appeal.

Also, AI's automation capabilities can streamline tasks that once required extensive manual effort. For example, using AI tools to generate meta descriptions or alt tags based on content context can save time and ensure consistency across web pages—a crucial aspect of maintaining a professional online presence.

Additionally, predictive analytics powered by machine learning algorithms allow SEO professionals to anticipate trends and adapt strategies accordingly. By examining patterns in user behavior data over time, businesses can identify emerging topics or shifts in interest before they gain mainstream traction. Take this example, an online clothing retailer might observe a growing interest in sustainable fashion searches. By adjusting their content strategy early in response to this trend, they position themselves as industry leaders rather than followers.

AI's influence also extends into personalization—a critical element of modern digital marketing strategies. Search engines are increasingly prioritizing personalized experiences based on users' past behaviors and preferences. If someone regularly searches for vegan recipes, their future search results will be tailored accordingly, showcasing options that are more relevant than generic ones. To capitalize on this trend, brands should leverage data analytics not just for optimizing existing content but also for creating new offerings that cater specifically to identified audience segments.

Consider real-world applications where businesses have effectively harnessed AI. A travel agency using chatbots powered by natural language processing (NLP) not only enhances user engagement but also gathers valuable data on customer inquiries and pain points. These insights can guide future content creation or service offerings—enabling the business to stay ahead of competitors who rely solely on static information.

However, while embracing AI brings numerous advantages, it's crucial to approach this technology with ethical considerations in mind. Transparency regarding data usage fosters trust— an invaluable asset in today's digital landscape where privacy concerns are paramount. Adhering to regulations like GDPR while utilizing AI tools can set your brand apart as a responsible leader in the market.

As we move through 2025 and beyond, those who successfully integrate artificial intelligence into their SEO practices will likely surpass competitors still adhering to traditional methods. The ability to swiftly adapt based on algorithm updates or emerging trends will define success—not just through improved visibility in search results but by genuinely engaging with and meeting user needs more efficiently than ever before.

In summary, embracing artificial intelligence is not merely about adopting new technology; it represents a fundamental shift in our approach to search engine optimization—transitioning from reactive measures to proactive strategies rooted in data-driven insights that reflect real user experiences and expectations. This transformation presents both challenges and opportunities for those willing to innovate continuously within this dynamic field of digital marketing.

Voice Search and Its Impact

Voice search is more than just a passing trend; it represents a fundamental shift in how users interact with technology and access information. As smart speakers and voice-activated devices become increasingly common, they are significantly transforming search behaviors. This evolution necessitates a fresh perspective on SEO strategies, urging marketers to rethink their approaches to content and keyword optimization.

Unlike traditional text searches that often rely on concise keywords, voice searches are inherently more conversational. Users tend to engage with their devices as if they are conversing with another person, which results in longer phrases and natural language patterns. Take this example, while someone might type "weather Paris" into a search engine, they are more likely to ask, "What's the weather like in Paris today?" Optimizing for voice search means anticipating these natural queries and structuring content to match.

To effectively navigate this new landscape, consider adopting a strategy focused on long-tail keywords. These phrases closely reflect how people naturally communicate. Tools like Answer the Public can be invaluable in this process, revealing common questions that individuals ask about specific topics. If you own a local bakery, for example, identifying queries such as "Where can I find gluten-free bread near me?" can inform your content creation efforts and help address specific customer needs.

In addition to keywords, structured data markup plays a crucial role in boosting visibility in voice search results. By implementing schema markup, you enable search engines to better understand the context of your content, increasing the likelihood that your website will be featured in rich answers or snippets—formats favored by voice assistants like Google Assistant and Amazon Alexa. Take this example, using schema for FAQs can allow immediate responses to user inquiries directly from the search engine results page (SERP), enhancing your chances of attracting traffic through voice searches.

A practical example of this can be seen with fitness centers creating FAQ pages that address common questions about memberships, classes, and health tips. By structuring this information with schema markup, when users ask about nearby fitness classes or healthy eating tips, your center's responses are more likely to be prioritized.

And, optimizing for local searches is essential since many voice queries are location-based. Keeping your Google My Business listing accurate and up-to-date can significantly improve your visibility when users inquire about nearby services. For example, if someone asks their device for the "best coffee shop close to me," having an optimized profile with relevant details like hours of operation and user reviews enhances your chances of being featured prominently in the response.

The influence of voice search also extends to user experience; speed and accessibility are critical factors. Users expect swift answers delivered seamlessly through their devices without any friction. Thus, ensuring that your website is mobile-friendly is not just best practice—it's essential for meeting the demands of voice search users who often rely on smartphones or smart home devices for immediate information.

As businesses adapt to these changes, experimenting with conversational content becomes increasingly vital. Blogs or articles written in a question-and-answer format not only resonate well with voice search algorithms but also create an engaging user experience for audiences seeking quick answers.

Consider Domino's Pizza as an example; they have successfully leveraged voice ordering through platforms like Amazon Alexa and Google Home. Customers can simply vocalize their orders without navigating through apps or websites—a seamless interaction that showcases the potential of integrating voice technology into business models.

However, as organizations embrace this shift towards voice-centric strategies, it is crucial not to overlook privacy concerns associated with data collection linked to these technologies. Being transparent about data usage fosters trust among users who may feel apprehensive about sharing personal information through voice-enabled devices.

To wrap things up, adapting SEO strategies for voice search involves not only technical adjustments but also a fundamental shift in our approach to content creation and user engagement. Those who proactively embrace this evolution will position themselves at the forefront of digital marketing innovation—effectively meeting consumer needs in this rapidly changing landscape while unlocking new opportunities for connection and growth.

Visual Search Integration

Visual search is transforming how users discover and interact with content online. As technology advances, so do the capabilities of search engines, leading to an increase in visual search functionalities that allow users to find information through images instead of text. This shift not only alters user behavior but also presents unique opportunities for SEO practitioners.

To enhance visibility in visual search, image optimization is crucial. High-quality images are essential, but it's equally important to use descriptive file names and alt text. Instead of naming an image "IMG1234.jpg," for instance, renaming it to "red-summer-dress.jpg" provides valuable context. Incorporating relevant keywords into the alt text further aids search engines in understanding the image content and increases the likelihood of appearing in image searches.

Implementing structured data markup for images is another effective strategy. Schema.org offers guidelines on tagging images appropriately, helping search engines interpret what your visuals represent. By enriching your images with structured data that includes details like product information or location context, you can improve visibility not only in standard image searches but also in visual searches performed on mobile devices.

Engaging visuals also play a vital role in capturing user attention. With platforms like Instagram and Pinterest prioritizing imagery, creating captivating content is essential. Consider developing a visually-driven blog or product gallery where high-resolution images not only attract viewers but also provide valuable information about your offerings—especially important in visually-driven industries like fashion or interior design.

A noteworthy example of successful visual search integration comes from furniture retailer Wayfair. They incorporated augmented reality (AR) features into their app, allowing customers to visualize products in their own homes before making a purchase. This innovative use of technology enhances user experience while effectively utilizing visual search by linking physical appearance with digital interaction.

Additionally, the placement of images within your website's architecture matters significantly. Ensure that key visuals are prominently displayed on product pages or landing sections where they can be easily accessed. A combination of appealing layouts and optimized images maximizes engagement potential and encourages sharing across social media platforms.

User-generated content (UGC) should also be considered as a way to enhance visual optimization. Encouraging customers to share pictures featuring your products on social media with specific brand-related hashtags creates authentic engagement while generating a wealth of visuals that may appear in searches related to your offerings.

As companies adapt to the rise of visual search technologies, analyzing competitors' approaches to visual assets becomes increasingly important. Tools like Google Images can help assess which types of visuals rank highly for specific keywords or topics within your niche. By studying the strategies of successful competitors, you can differentiate yourself through innovative imagery that stands out.

However, amid these advancements lies the essential focus on accessibility. Not all users navigate websites effortlessly; therefore, ensuring that all imagery adheres to accessibility standards is critical for inclusivity. Image descriptions should fulfill both SEO requirements and support users relying on screen readers or other assistive technologies.

In summary, optimizing for visual search involves a multifaceted strategy that blends technical adjustments with creative enhancements aimed at engaging users through compelling visuals. As this trend continues to evolve, businesses willing to innovate will find themselves well-positioned within the digital landscape—where every image tells a story resonating deeply with their audience's aspirations and needs.

Semantic Search and Its Implications

Semantic search is fundamentally transforming user interactions with search engines, moving away from keyword-centric queries to a deeper understanding of the intent behind those queries. This shift is driven by advanced algorithms and

AI technologies that prioritize contextual meaning over simple word matching. For example, when a user searches for "best places to eat near me," a semantic search engine interprets this as a request for nearby restaurant recommendations rather than merely retrieving text that contains those keywords.

One significant consequence of semantic search is the emergence of conversational queries. As voice search gains popularity, users are increasingly adopting a more natural language style in their interactions with devices. Rather than relying on fragmented phrases, they pose complete questions or make statements, such as "What's the best Italian restaurant nearby?" This evolution necessitates a reevaluation of keyword strategies; SEO professionals must now focus on long-tail keywords and phrases that mirror everyday speech.

To effectively navigate this change, marketers should invest time in understanding user intent through thorough audience research. Crafting content that addresses common questions or pain points within your niche is crucial. Take this example, a travel blog might create an in-depth guide titled "10 Tips for Traveling in Italy" instead of concentrating solely on generic keyword-rich articles. The closer your content aligns with user needs, the better it will perform according to semantic search criteria.

In addition to understanding user intent, leveraging structured data can significantly enhance visibility in this new landscape. By implementing schema markup, businesses help search engines better understand the context of their content, enabling them to deliver more relevant results based on user intent. For example, a recipe website that employs structured data can display rich snippets like cooking times and ingredient lists directly in search results, attracting clicks from users seeking quick information.

The importance of context also extends to local SEO efforts. When users conduct searches with local intent—such as "coffee shops open now"—search engines consider various contextual factors, including location and recent search history. To improve local visibility, businesses should optimize their Google My Business profiles and ensure consistency in their Name, Address, and Phone Number (NAP) across directories. Additionally, incorporating local keywords and engaging with customer reviews can further strengthen their online presence.

Recognizing the implications of semantic search leads us to reflect on its impact on content creation itself. High-quality content should address not only what users are searching for but also why they are searching for it. For example, a healthcare website focusing on diabetes management could go beyond listing treatment options by offering articles that explore lifestyle changes for patients or answer common questions about living with diabetes. This approach fosters authority and trust while resonating deeply with users' concerns.

And, user engagement metrics are increasingly influencing rankings within semantic search frameworks. Search engines analyze how users interact with your content—such as time spent on the page, click-through rates, and bounce rates—to assess relevance and quality. Crafting compelling headlines and meta descriptions is essential for enticing clicks; however, the content must deliver real value to keep users engaged once they arrive at your site.

A notable case study illustrating these principles is HubSpot's blog strategy. Their posts often begin with questions derived from user searches—like "How can I improve my email marketing?"—and provide thorough answers paired with actionable advice and examples. This approach not only attracts organic traffic but also positions HubSpot as an industry authority through its relevance and value.

As semantic technologies continue to advance, so too will the expectations surrounding SEO practices. Embracing this paradigm shift is crucial; businesses willing to adapt will thrive amid ongoing digital transformation. In this dynamic landscape, a proactive strategy that combines deep audience insights with robust technical implementations will give organizations a competitive edge.

understanding the nuances of semantic search empowers marketers to develop strategies that resonate on multiple levels—offering immediate answers while fostering long-term relationships with audiences grounded in trust and relevance. It's an exciting frontier where human behavior meets cutting-edge technology—a fertile ground for innovation and success in an increasingly competitive environment.

The Role of Data and Analytics

In 2025, data and analytics have become essential components of effective SEO strategies, allowing marketers to gain a deeper understanding of their audiences and tailor their approaches accordingly. By integrating data-driven insights into SEO practices, businesses can significantly enhance their connections with users and optimize their digital presence. To fully leverage the potential of SEO, it's vital to explore the pivotal role that data and analytics play in shaping strategies and driving performance.

Central to this evolution is the capacity to collect, analyze, and interpret large volumes of data. Tools like Google Analytics and various SEO platforms provide valuable metrics that inform strategic decisions. For example, monitoring organic traffic, bounce rates, and conversion rates enables marketers to assess the effectiveness of their content. Analyzing these metrics helps identify which pages attract visitors and which ones fail to engage them effectively. A thorough understanding of user behavior directs optimization efforts, ensuring that resources are allocated where they will have the most impact.

Consider a practical scenario: an e-commerce site discovers a high bounce rate on its product pages. A closer look at the analytics reveals that while many users arrive at these pages, they often leave without making a purchase. This insight triggers a review of various factors—such as page load speed, product descriptions, and pricing strategies. By addressing these issues informed by data, the site can enhance user experience and ultimately increase conversion rates.

User segmentation is another powerful application of data analytics in SEO. By categorizing audiences based on demographics, interests, or behavioral patterns, marketers can create targeted content that resonates with specific groups. Take this example, if analytics indicate that younger users engage more with video content, a brand might focus on developing engaging video tutorials or product demos tailored to that demographic. This personalized approach not only boosts engagement but also fosters brand loyalty through relevant experiences.

A/B testing further exemplifies how analytical insights can optimize website elements. By experimenting with different headlines, images, or calls to action (CTAs), marketers can determine which variations drive higher engagement or conversions. For example, an online retailer might test two versions of a product page—one featuring a bold "Buy Now" button and the other a "Learn More" option. Analyzing user interactions with both versions clarifies which design resonates better with visitors.

The impact of analytics extends beyond user behavior; it also informs keyword strategies. Tools like SEMrush and Ahrefs help marketers track keyword performance over time and uncover new opportunities based on emerging search trends. Take this example, if data indicates a surge in searches for "eco-friendly packaging" within a specific niche market, businesses can adapt their content strategy to include this trend—creating optimized blog posts or product pages before competitors do.

Local SEO efforts also benefit significantly from data insights. Tools like Google My Business Insights provide critical information about how customers discover businesses in their local area—whether through direct searches or related queries. Understanding these metrics allows businesses to refine their local strategies; for example, if many users find a business via mobile searches but not desktop ones, it may indicate the need for improved mobile site performance.

Additionally, social media metrics play a crucial role in shaping contemporary SEO strategies. Engaging content shared across platforms can enhance visibility and drive traffic back to websites. Monitoring which posts receive the most interaction reveals what types of content resonate with audiences—and consequently informs SEO priorities.

The significance of this data-centric approach cannot be overstated; organizations that effectively leverage analytics consistently outperform those that do not. Take Amazon, for example: their adept use of data analytics enables them to dynamically personalize shopping experiences based on individual browsing habits and past purchases. This level of insight not only drives sales but also elevates customer satisfaction—a key factor in maintaining a competitive edge.

It's essential to remember that data analysis transcends mere number collection; it's about weaving a narrative through those numbers. The insights gleaned from analytics must translate into actionable strategies grounded in real-world contexts. Presenting findings in visually appealing reports facilitates quick comprehension among stakeholders—aligning teams toward shared goals.

In summary, incorporating robust data analysis into SEO practices empowers marketers to make informed decisions that markedly enhance performance. From refining keyword strategies to optimizing user experiences based on behavioral insights, data serves as both compass and map in navigating the intricate digital landscape of 2025. Embracing this analytical mindset not only yields better results but also positions brands as leaders in an ever-evolving marketplace—a crucial advantage as competition intensifies and consumer expectations continue to rise.

Current Search Engine Market Share

Understanding the current search engine market share is essential for anyone involved in SEO. It provides context for developing effective strategies and positioning against competitors. As we look ahead to 2025, the landscape has undergone significant changes, reflecting the growing influence of platforms beyond traditional giants like Google. This evolution is not just about shifting numbers; it highlights changing user preferences and technological advancements that are transforming our interactions with search engines.

Google continues to be a dominant player, commanding a large portion of the market share. Its sophisticated algorithms and regular updates aimed at enhancing user experience make it a focal point for marketers who tailor their strategies around Google's guidelines. Take this example, Google's emphasis on E-A-T (Expertise, Authoritativeness, Trustworthiness) means businesses must produce high-quality content that adheres to these principles. Those that excel in these areas often enjoy greater visibility in search results.

Yet, the rise of alternative search engines cannot be ignored. Bing, for example, has made impressive gains by attracting users who appreciate its unique features, such as enhanced image search and seamless integration with Microsoft products. Recent analytics indicate that Bing's market share has surpassed 10%, largely due to users seeking a different experience from Google. For businesses looking to diversify their traffic sources, optimizing for Bing by understanding its ranking factors and user engagement metrics can be a strategic move.

Emerging platforms like DuckDuckGo are also reshaping the search landscape by appealing to privacy-conscious users who prefer not to be tracked by traditional search engines.

DuckDuckGo's growth underscores the increasing importance of data privacy in user experience. This trend encourages brands to rethink how they present information and engage with audiences that prioritize anonymity online. To effectively reach this audience segment, creating content that respects user privacy while still providing value can enhance visibility on platforms like DuckDuckGo.

Social media is carving out its own niche in the search space as well. Features like Instagram's Explore tab and Pinterest's visual discovery tools have become popular avenues for product searches and inspiration-seeking behaviors. Businesses must adapt their SEO strategies to include social media optimization; for example, brands can optimize Pinterest pins with relevant keywords while focusing on visually appealing content to drive traffic from these platforms.

The impact of voice search is another critical factor worth considering. With the proliferation of smart devices—from phones to home assistants—search queries are becoming increasingly conversational. Studies indicate that over 30% of searches are now voice-activated, necessitating a reevaluation of keyword strategies to incorporate natural language phrases rather than rigidly adhering to traditional keyword structures. Tailoring content for voice search involves emphasizing long-tail keywords and FAQs that reflect how people naturally speak.

And, the integration of AI-driven technologies into search engine functionalities marks a noteworthy trend. Search engines now employ AI algorithms not only for ranking but also for better understanding user intent. This shift means businesses must continually adjust their SEO tactics based on evolving AI capabilities; grasping how machine learning influences search results can provide a competitive edge.

Amazon exemplifies effective use of market share insights through data analytics and an understanding of customer preferences within its ecosystem. By dominating e-commerce and serving as a primary product discovery tool for many consumers, Amazon challenges traditional search engines in new ways.

As you evaluate your own SEO strategies in light of these market dynamics, adopting a flexible approach is vital—embracing diversity across multiple channels, whether through traditional search engines or innovative platforms gaining traction today. What you should know is clear: staying informed about current market shares will empower you to develop strategies that resonate with your target audience while navigating an ever-evolving digital landscape.

To maximize your SEO efforts moving forward, consider conducting regular audits of your market positioning across various platforms and adjusting your tactics accordingly. Whether focusing on content creation tailored for Google or optimizing product listings for Amazon or social media searches, having a comprehensive understanding of your traffic sources will enable you to make informed decisions that effectively drive growth and visibility in 2025 and beyond.

Search Engines Beyond Google

The idea of search engines encompasses much more than just Google. As the digital landscape evolves, it is essential to recognize the variety of search platforms that are transforming how users find information and make decisions. This shift goes beyond competition; it represents a fundamental change in consumer behavior and preferences, which significantly impacts your SEO strategy.

Bing, often seen as a secondary option, has been steadily carving out its own niche. With enhanced features like image search and integration with Microsoft's suite of applications, Bing is gaining market share. For businesses looking to capitalize on this opportunity, understanding Bing's unique ranking factors is crucial. Unlike Google's algorithm, which prioritizes backlinks and content quality, Bing places greater emphasis on social signals and user engagement. Therefore, strategies that enhance social media interactions can improve visibility on Bing and attract its user base.

Meanwhile, privacy-focused search engines like DuckDuckGo are gaining traction as more users seek alternatives that prioritize data security. The appeal of these platforms lies in their straightforward approach: no tracking or personalized ads means users feel safer while searching online. This trend encourages marketers to create transparent and straightforward content that delivers value without compromising user privacy. By aligning with these values, brands can effectively connect with an audience increasingly wary of traditional data collection methods.

Social media platforms also significantly influence search behavior. Instagram and Pinterest are at the forefront of visual search functionality, with users often turning to these platforms for inspiration or product discovery rather than traditional search engines. Businesses should optimize their presence on these channels by incorporating relevant keywords into their posts and ensuring visuals are captivating enough to grab attention quickly. Take this example, Pinterest allows for the integration of rich pins that can drive traffic back to your site when properly optimized.

Voice search represents another notable shift in how people interact with technology. As smart speakers become common in homes and on devices, voice-activated queries are reshaping content creation strategies. It is important to move beyond traditional keyword tactics and consider phrasing that reflects natural speech patterns. Long-tail keywords and question-based formats will resonate more effectively with voice searches—optimizing FAQs on your website not only addresses this trend but also answers common user queries directly.

The rise of AI technologies within search functionalities cannot be overlooked either. Search engines increasingly employ AI not only to refine algorithms but also to gain deeper insights into user intent than ever before. This evolution necessitates continuous adaptation from marketers; staying informed about AI developments allows you to refine your content strategies effectively. For example, leveraging machine learning analytics can reveal how different audiences interact with your content across various platforms.

Consider Amazon—a prime example of a platform that transcends traditional definitions of a search engine by focusing heavily on product discovery through data-driven strategies. With a nuanced understanding of customer preferences, Amazon optimizes its interface as a dynamic tool for consumers seeking new products daily.

This multifaceted view of the search engine landscape underscores the importance of diversifying across multiple platforms for an effective SEO strategy moving into 2025. Regularly revisiting your approach ensures you engage effectively with users regardless of where they choose to seek information—whether through conventional search engines or emerging technologies reshaping online discovery.

By embracing this diversity and remaining adaptable in your tactics—whether enhancing Google-focused content or optimizing Amazon listings—you position yourself favorably within the ever-changing digital arena. Informed actions based on current market dynamics will not only enhance visibility but also foster deeper connections with varied audience segments across all available channels.

As you reflect on these insights, remember: developing robust SEO practices requires an ongoing commitment to understanding emerging trends and behaviors within each platform's user base. This proactive approach will distinguish you as an innovative leader in the world of SEO as we advance into 2025 and beyond.

CHAPTER 3:
KEYWORD RESEARCH FOR A NEW ERA

Fundamentals of Keyword Research

K eyword research is the cornerstone of an effective SEO strategy. It goes beyond merely selecting a list of words to sprinkle throughout your content; it involves understanding the intent behind those words and how they align with your audience's needs. In today's fast-evolving digital landscape, where user behavior shifts continuously, getting keyword research right can significantly boost your visibility and help you connect with the right audience at the right moment.

To begin, it's essential to recognize that keywords reflect user intent. People search for specific information based on their needs—whether they are looking to solve a problem, seek advice, or make a purchase. This distinction among informational, navigational, and transactional queries is crucial for shaping your keyword strategy. For example, someone searching for "best running shoes" likely intends to buy, while another searching "how to choose running shoes" seeks guidance.

To effectively capture this diverse range of intent, start with comprehensive brainstorming sessions. Gather insights from various sources: customer inquiries, social media conversations, forums like Reddit or Quora, and competitor analyses can reveal trending topics and frequently asked questions within your niche. Tools such as AnswerThePublic can help visualize questions related to keywords that users are asking across different platforms, providing invaluable context about what your audience is genuinely interested in.

Once you have compiled a list of potential keywords, it's time to utilize tools designed for deeper analysis. Google Keyword Planner remains a staple resource for discovering search volume and competition metrics. However, don't overlook other robust tools like SEMrush or Ahrefs that offer rich insights into keyword difficulty and potential traffic estimates. These platforms enable you to analyze how competitors rank for specific keywords and identify gaps in your own strategy.

It's also important to consider the value of long-tail keywords. While broader terms may seem appealing due to high search volumes, they often come with stiff competition and unclear user intent. Long-tail keywords—phrases containing three or more words—tend to attract more qualified traffic because they cater to specific queries. Take this example, "best trail running shoes for flat feet" targets a niche audience ready to convert rather than general inquiries that may lead nowhere.

After identifying promising keywords, delve into user intent more deeply using Latent Semantic Indexing (LSI) keywords —terms semantically related to your primary keyword that help Google understand context better. For example, if your main keyword is "vegan recipes," relevant LSI keywords might include "plant-based cooking," "dairy-free meals," or "easy vegan dishes." Integrating these into your content enriches its relevance and broadens its reach in search results.

Competitor analysis should also play a vital role in your

keyword research process. Use tools like SpyFu or Moz's Keyword Explorer to identify which keywords drive traffic to competitors' websites. Analyzing their top-performing pages not only uncovers new keyword opportunities but also provides insight into how they structure their content around these terms— a critical consideration as you strategize your own content approach.

A practical step forward is creating a keyword matrix—a document that organizes keywords based on categories such as buyer persona stages (awareness, consideration, decision), content types (blog posts, product pages), and search intent (informational vs transactional). This matrix serves as a roadmap for creating targeted content that aligns seamlessly with both user intent and business goals.

Once you've established your strategy, prioritize high-value keywords based on their alignment with the content themes on your site. For each piece of content you create or optimize, ensure it targets one primary keyword while naturally integrating secondary LSI keywords throughout the text. Additionally, enhance title tags and meta descriptions with carefully chosen keywords; these elements are essential for improving click-through rates from search results.

Keep in mind that keyword research is not a one-time task but an ongoing commitment. Regularly revisiting keyword performance allows you to adapt quickly when trends shift or new opportunities arise—be it seasonal spikes in interest or emerging topics within your niche that gain traction unexpectedly.

As you refine this critical aspect of SEO strategy moving into 2025, stay informed about evolving tools and techniques within the field of keyword research itself. Technologies driven by artificial intelligence are increasingly capable of rapidly analyzing vast datasets; leveraging these advancements could provide significant advantages over competitors who stick to outdated methodologies.

In summary, understanding the fundamentals of keyword research extends beyond merely identifying terms—it requires an iterative process grounded in audience insight and market dynamics. By skillfully blending user intent with strategic execution informed by data-driven analysis, you'll position yourself ahead of the curve in today's competitive digital marketing landscape. Embrace this foundational work; it will yield significant dividends as you develop effective SEO strategies tailored precisely to meet user needs.

Tools and Platforms for Keyword Analysis

Keyword analysis is a fundamental element of any effective SEO strategy. By understanding the available tools and platforms, marketers can uncover opportunities, assess competition, and optimize content more efficiently. A closer look at these keyword analysis tools reveals their functionalities and how they can be leveraged to develop a robust keyword strategy tailored to specific goals.

One of the most recognized tools in this space is Google Keyword Planner. Primarily designed for advertisers, it provides valuable insights into keyword volumes, forecasts, and competition levels. To begin using Google Keyword Planner, simply enter a few seed keywords related to your niche. The tool will then generate a comprehensive list of related keywords along with their average monthly search volumes and suggested bids for advertising. This information is crucial for identifying high-traffic keywords while keeping budget constraints in mind if paid search is part of your strategy.

Another powerful option is SEMrush, which extends beyond basic keyword analysis to offer a comprehensive suite of SEO tools. With SEMrush, you can explore keyword trends and conduct competitive analysis simultaneously. By entering a competitor's domain, you can see the keywords they rank for, their positions in search results, and estimated traffic. This capability enables you to pinpoint gaps in your own strategy by targeting keywords that competitors may be neglecting. For example, if you operate in the health sector and discover that competitors rank highly for "holistic wellness," you might consider creating content focused on niche variations such as "holistic wellness practices for busy professionals" to appeal to a specific audience segment.

Ahrefs has also gained significant traction among SEO professionals thanks to its robust features. Its keyword explorer function provides important metrics like Keyword Difficulty (KD) scores and Click-Through Rate (CTR) estimations. The KD score indicates how competitive a keyword is based on the strength of the top-ranking pages for that term. Take this example, if you're interested in "digital marketing strategies" but encounter a high KD score suggesting fierce competition, you could shift your focus to more specific long-tail keywords like "digital marketing strategies for small businesses." Long-tail keywords often lead to higher conversion rates as they target users who are further along in the buying process.

For those new to keyword research, Ubersuggest offers an intuitive interface that simplifies the process. Developed by Neil Patel, Ubersuggest provides keyword suggestions along with data on search volume and seasonal trends. One standout feature is its "Content Ideas" section, which showcases top-performing content based on specific keywords. This helps marketers understand what type of content resonates with audiences and inspires them to create similar or improved articles.

In addition to traditional tools, social media platforms provide insights into trending topics and keywords through their analytics features. For example, Twitter reveals trending hashtags relevant to your industry, guiding content creation to align with current interests. If "sustainable fashion" trends on Twitter during a particular season, consider developing content that explores sustainable brands or offers tips on eco-friendly shopping.

Google Trends is another valuable resource that allows you to analyze the popularity of search queries over time. This tool is particularly useful for determining whether a topic has enduring interest or if it's merely a passing trend. By entering a broad term like "remote work," you may observe spikes in interest that correspond with global events or seasonal changes —insights that can inform timely content production.

By integrating multiple tools into your keyword analysis process, you can create a more comprehensive strategy. For example, use Google Keyword Planner for foundational research while supplementing it with insights from SEMrush and Ahrefs for competitive advantage and deeper metrics. Each platform enhances your understanding in unique ways— whether through user-generated data from social media or long-term trends visible via Google Trends.

With these resources at your disposal, crafting an effective keyword strategy becomes more straightforward and data-driven. By continuously refining your approach based on insights from these tools, you'll improve your ability to attract targeted traffic and produce content that meets your audience's needs. incorporating advanced analytics into your keyword research will elevate your SEO efforts and significantly impact overall digital marketing success.

Understanding User Intent

Understanding user intent is crucial in the ever-evolving landscape of SEO, where search engines increasingly prioritize relevant and personalized results. It's not just about pinpointing keywords; it's about grasping what users genuinely seek when they enter a query. This understanding not only shapes content strategy but can also mean the difference between securing a spot on the first page of search results or being lost in obscurity.

User intent typically falls into three categories: informational, navigational, and transactional. Each category serves a distinct purpose and necessitates tailored content strategies. For example, a person searching for "best digital cameras" is likely seeking detailed comparisons or reviews—indicative of informational intent. In contrast, someone searching for "buy digital camera" demonstrates transactional intent, signaling readiness to make a purchase. Recognizing these nuances allows marketers to align their content effectively with user needs.

Take this example, if your website specializes in photography gear, understanding that the term "best digital cameras" reflects informational intent suggests the creation of comprehensive comparison articles or guides. Titles like "Top 10 Digital Cameras for Beginners" or "Expert Reviews of 2025's Best DSLR Cameras" would be appropriate. On the other hand, for transactional queries, optimizing product pages with clear calls-to-action and streamlined checkout processes becomes essential to facilitate purchases.

To explore user intent further, tools like AnswerThePublic can be invaluable in revealing common questions and phrases related to your target keywords. By entering "digital camera," you can access a visual map of user queries such as "What is the best digital camera for photography?" These insights not only help identify potential content topics but also illuminate the language and phrasing that resonate with your audience.

Additionally, analyzing search engine results pages (SERPs) offers critical context about user intent. If a keyword generates featured snippets, FAQs, or video content among its top results, it indicates that users are interested in diverse formats of information on that topic. Take this example, if videos dominate SERPs for "how to take better photos," it suggests that users might prefer visual instructions over lengthy text articles.

Another important consideration is the evolution of user behavior over time. The same keyword can reflect different intents depending on current trends or events. Take this example, during holiday seasons or major shopping events like

Black Friday, search queries with transactional intent tend to surge as consumers look for deals. Staying attuned to these shifts allows marketers to adjust their strategies dynamically, creating timely content that captures interest precisely when it peaks.

And, utilizing analytics tools such as Google Analytics enables you to track how users engage with your content once they arrive at your site. Metrics like bounce rate and average session duration can reveal whether users find the information they seek or leave quickly. A high bounce rate may indicate a disconnect between user expectations and the content provided; refining these pages based on behavioral insights can better satisfy user intents.

Personalization is also becoming increasingly vital in aligning with user intent. As algorithms grow more sophisticated, understanding the demographic and psychographic profiles of your audience enables you to craft tailored experiences. For example, leveraging data segmentation allows for personalized email campaigns based on past searches or purchases— encouraging repeat visits and enhancing customer loyalty.

Creating user personas that reflect different segments of your audience based on their intentions can be a beneficial practice. By categorizing visitors into groups such as "research-focused buyers" or "immediate purchase seekers," you can develop specific content strategies tailored to their unique needs and desires.

In the dynamic world of SEO, ongoing adaptation is essential; therefore, regularly reassessing your understanding of user intent is crucial for sustained success. Staying ahead requires not only analyzing current trends but also anticipating future changes in consumer behavior influenced by technological advancements or societal shifts.

focusing on user intent transforms SEO from a tactical exercise into a strategic endeavor rooted in an understanding of human behavior. By developing content that addresses the genuine needs of your audience—whether informational or transactional—you position yourself to attract qualified traffic while fostering meaningful connections with users who will return time and again for valuable insights tailored just for them.

Long-Tail vs. Short-Tail Keywords

Long-tail keywords have become increasingly essential in the SEO toolkit, as they address more specific search queries. Unlike short-tail keywords, which are typically broad and highly competitive, long-tail keywords generally attract lower search volumes but offer greater conversion potential. Take this example, while the term "digital cameras" may draw a vast audience, a phrase like "best digital cameras for wildlife photography under (500" targets a niche market with clearer intent. By focusing on these longer phrases, marketers can connect with users who are closer to making purchasing decisions.

The difference between long-tail and short-tail keywords goes beyond theory; it has practical implications for content creation and marketing strategies. Short-tail keywords can drive significant traffic but often face intense competition due to their general nature. On the other hand, long-tail keywords enable businesses to compete more effectively in less crowded spaces. This advantage is especially beneficial for smaller brands or newcomers who might struggle to rank against established competitors.

Consider the case of a local bakery. If they optimize for the short-tail keyword "cake," they encounter fierce competition from global brands and larger bakery chains. However, by targeting long-tail variations such as "organic wedding cake delivery in San Francisco," they can attract customers specifically looking for those services in their area. This level of specificity increases engagement potential since these users are further along in their decision-making process.

Keyword research plays a crucial role in uncovering effective long-tail opportunities. Tools like SEMrush and Ahrefs provide valuable insights into search volume, keyword difficulty, and related phrases that can guide your strategy. For example, if your analysis shows that "gluten-free birthday cakes" has considerable interest but low competition, creating focused content around this phrase could yield substantial organic traffic with minimal effort.

To seamlessly incorporate long-tail keywords into your content, it's essential to write naturally around these phrases while providing genuine value to readers. A blog post titled "Top 5 Gluten-Free Birthday Cake Recipes" not only targets the keyword directly but also offers actionable information that meets potential customers' needs, enhancing user engagement metrics.

As you develop content centered on long-tail keywords, consider user intent: what questions or problems does your target audience have? Addressing these concerns through detailed guides or FAQs can further elevate your relevance and authority on the topic. Implementing structured data markup can also boost visibility in search results by displaying rich snippets that attract users browsing through search engine results pages (SERPs).

And, long-tail keywords align well with the shift in consumer behavior toward voice search technology. As more users rely on voice assistants like Siri or Google Assistant, queries tend to become more conversational and specific compared to traditional text searches. Phrases like "find vegan cake recipes near me" exemplify typical voice searches where adopting long-tail strategies is crucial for capturing this growing demographic.

However, it's important to strike a balance between focusing on long-tail keywords and incorporating short-tail keywords into your strategy. Utilizing short-tail terms at strategic points can drive broader traffic while creating an environment where longer phrases engage visitors who are ready to convert.

successful SEO today hinges on this balance—leveraging both types of keywords enables you to craft robust content strategies that address various stages of the customer journey. The true power of combining long- and short-tail keywords lies in understanding their unique roles within your overall SEO efforts and continually analyzing performance metrics to refine your approach over time.

Emphasizing long-tail optimization is not just about attracting clicks; it's about building authentic connections with users who find exactly what they're searching for at that moment— a vital factor driving conversion success in today's competitive online landscape. By adopting this nuanced perspective, you can transform keyword strategy from a basic framework into an advanced practice tailored to effectively meet diverse user needs.

The Power of Latent Semantic Indexing (LSI)

Incorporating LSI keywords into your content strategy allows you to tap into a deeper understanding that enhances both readability and relevance. For example, when writing about "digital marketing," using related terms such as "SEO," "content marketing," "social media strategies," and tools like "Google Analytics" or "HubSpot" enriches the text. This not only aligns with what search engines seek but also provides readers with a more comprehensive insight into the subject matter.

The practical application of LSI begins with thorough keyword research. Tools like Google's Keyword Planner and Ubersuggest can help you uncover not only primary keywords but also related terms that function as LSI keywords. Take this example, when researching an article on "healthy eating," you might find relevant terms such as "nutritional value," "meal prep," or "whole foods." By seamlessly incorporating these keywords throughout your content, you signal to search engines that your article thoroughly covers the topic.

To illustrate LSI in action, consider a fitness website creating an article titled "10 Tips for Effective Weight Loss." Rather than focusing solely on the phrase "weight loss," they could enhance their content by including related phrases like "caloric deficit," "exercise routines," and "meal planning." This layered approach not only broadens the article's reach but also increases its chances of appearing in various searches related to weight management.

Optimizing content for LSI involves more than just keyword density; it requires a natural flow and engaging language. Search engines are becoming increasingly adept at evaluating user behavior metrics—such as time spent on page, bounce rate, and interaction levels—to determine content quality. Therefore, while incorporating LSI keywords is important, ensuring that your writing flows organically is equally crucial. This approach not only supports SEO efforts but also enhances the reader's experience.

Understanding how user queries evolve over time is another critical aspect of effective content strategy. Users don't always type exact phrases; they often utilize variations or synonyms during their searches. Take this example, someone looking for information on "dog training" may also search for "puppy obedience" or "canine behavior." By recognizing these variations, you can adapt your content strategy to incorporate these synonyms into your broader keyword plan.

Additionally, integrating LSI into structured data markup can improve how search engines interpret your content's context. Using schema.org markup clarifies relationships between different elements within your pages, providing extra cues about how various components relate to each other. This practice can enhance visibility in search engine results pages (SERPs) through rich snippets.

As voice search continues to gain traction, leveraging LSI becomes even more essential. Users tend to phrase their questions in a conversational tone when using voice assistants; thus, incorporating variations of keywords becomes crucial for effectively matching these queries. A person might ask, "How do I train my puppy?" instead of simply searching for "dog training." Crafting responses that address these specific inquiries while integrating relevant phrases can significantly boost your rankings.

Finally, monitoring performance metrics related to LSI usage is vital for refining your strategy. Analyzing which related terms drive traffic can inform future content creation and keyword selection efforts. Tools like Google Search Console provide insights into how users discover your pages through organic search—this information can help identify effective LSI keywords worth exploring further.

Embracing Latent Semantic Indexing is not just a tactic; it represents a holistic approach to enhancing SEO effectiveness by recognizing the nuances of language and user intent. As search algorithms continue to evolve toward prioritizing contextual understanding over mere keyword matching, integrating this powerful technique will be essential for maintaining relevance in an increasingly competitive digital landscape. It transforms basic keyword targeting into a sophisticated strategy aimed at delivering genuine value—resulting not just in clicks but also in meaningful engagement from users seeking information that truly resonates with them.

Competitor Analysis for Keywords

To effectively compete in the dynamic world of SEO, conducting a thorough analysis of your competitors' keywords has become an essential strategy. This process not only reveals which keywords are driving traffic to your competitors but also uncovers opportunities for you to strategically position your own content in the market. By understanding what works for others, you can gain valuable insights that enhance your own efforts, helping you remain relevant and competitive.

Start your analysis by identifying your primary competitors within your niche. Utilize tools like Ahrefs or SEMrush to compile a list of websites that are vying for the same audience. For example, if you're running a travel blog focused on adventure tourism, it's vital to pinpoint other travel blogs or websites that share similar themes and target demographics. These sites will serve as benchmarks against which you can measure your keyword performance.

Once you've identified your competitors, explore their keyword strategies in depth. Tools such as Moz's Keyword Explorer or Ubersuggest allow you to see which keywords generate the most traffic for them. By entering a competitor's domain, you can uncover high-ranking keywords that may be underutilized or overlooked by others. This exploration can help identify gaps in your own keyword strategy, presenting opportunities for growth.

Take this example, if a competitor ranks highly for "best hiking trails," but has low visibility on related phrases like "eco-friendly hiking gear," this indicates an opportunity for you to create content that addresses this gap. Developing articles around these related terms not only diversifies your content but also positions you as an authority on eco-friendly outdoor activities.

In addition to identifying high-potential keywords, it's important to analyze the search intent behind them. Understanding how competitors address various intents— whether informational, navigational, or transactional—can guide how you tailor your content. If a competitor's page on "adventure travel tips" ranks well but garners little engagement compared to "top adventure travel destinations," it suggests that users might prefer more straightforward lists or recommendations over broader guides. Adapting your content strategy based on such insights can lead to higher engagement and improved rankings.

Competitor analysis should also involve examining what

doesn't work for them. Analyzing their unsuccessful keywords can provide valuable lessons about what audiences may find unappealing or irrelevant at any given moment. For example, if a competitor heavily promoted "affordable luxury cruises" but saw poor performance and high bounce rates, it may indicate that the target audience is currently more interested in budget travel tips rather than upscale options.

In addition to keyword performance, consider how competitors structure their pages—titles, headings, and meta descriptions—and how they optimize these elements with targeted keywords. Tools like Screaming Frog can help audit the optimization of these components across competitive sites. A comparative analysis of title tags reveals not only keyword placement but also offers insights into crafting compelling titles that attract clicks while aligning with user search intent.

Also, don't overlook social media engagement when evaluating competitors' keyword strategies. Platforms like BuzzSumo enable you to see how often articles from those websites are shared and discussed online. This data highlights topics that resonate with audiences and should inform your own content approach.

Another key aspect is backlinks; analyzing where competitors earn their links can uncover potential partnership opportunities for you as well. Tools like Majestic or LinkResearchTools assist in this analysis by showing which authoritative sites link back to competitor articles based on specific keywords or topics. If many reputable sites link back to a competitor's piece on "sustainable travel practices," targeting similar themes may encourage those platforms to link back to your related content.

By synthesizing insights from both successful and unsuccessful keyword strategies alongside an understanding of user intent and backlink profiles, you can create a comprehensive keyword strategy that is clear and actionable. Formulate new strategies based on concrete data rather than mere assumptions; prioritize long-tail keywords where competition is lower but demand remains strong—this often results in higher conversion rates as visitors engage more deeply with niche-specific content.

Regularly revisiting this analysis keeps you agile in an industry characterized by constant change. Updating tactics as new trends emerge ensures that you maintain relevance in search results over time.

In summary, thorough competitor analysis goes beyond mere observation; it empowers SEO strategists by illuminating previously unnoticed pathways within their niches while providing clarity around audience behavior dynamics involved in successful targeting strategies in today's complex digital marketing landscape.

Utilizing Google Trends

Harnessing the power of Google Trends can significantly elevate your keyword strategy and enhance your overall SEO effectiveness. This tool serves not merely as a repository of data but as a vital compass that navigates the constantly changing landscape of search behavior. By tapping into the insights offered by Google Trends, you can fine-tune your content strategy to closely align with what users are actively searching for, ensuring that your website remains both relevant and authoritative.

Start by investigating the search volume trends for keywords specific to your niche. Take this example, if you operate in the fitness sector, entering "home workouts" into Google Trends will unveil patterns over time. You may notice spikes in searches during January when people are motivated by New Year's resolutions. This understanding enables you to time your content marketing efforts effectively, such as launching an article on home workout tips just as interest peaks.

Another valuable application of Google Trends is the ability to compare multiple keywords side by side. Imagine you're deciding between focusing on "keto diet" or "paleo diet." By contrasting these terms within Google Trends, you can gauge their relative popularity over a set timeframe. If you find that the keto diet consistently outshines paleo, it would be prudent to center your blog posts or videos around keto-related topics, thereby reaching a wider audience eager for that information.

Regional insights provided by Google Trends are equally invaluable. The tool allows you to identify where certain keywords are most popular geographically. For example, if you run a local bakery and discover that "gluten-free cupcakes" is trending in your area but not in other regions, this could present a lucrative opportunity for targeted promotions or specialized product offerings. Tailoring your marketing strategies based on localized data fosters deeper connections with potential customers nearby.

Digging deeper into Google Trends also enables you to analyze related queries that may emerge alongside your primary keywords. These suggested searches often reveal emerging topics or shifts in user interest that might not yet be widely acknowledged. Take this example, if users searching for "sustainable fashion" increasingly look up "upcycled clothing," this trend indicates an evolving consumer mindset that you can leverage by creating timely and relevant content addressing this new interest.

Visualizing data trends through Google Trends can also help convey compelling narratives about your brand's relevance to stakeholders or clients. When proposing a new marketing strategy or showcasing past successes, highlighting spikes in interest for specific topics or products reinforces how well-informed decisions can lead to positive outcomes.

Incorporating seasonal trends is another critical element of effective utilization. If data indicates that searches for "summer skincare tips" surge every spring, planning posts around these times ensures you're delivering timely and valuable information when users are actively seeking it out. This proactive approach can lead to improved engagement rates as users find exactly what they need at just the right moment.

However, it's essential not only to extract insights from Google Trends but also to act on them decisively. As trends evolve, so should your focus areas within your SEO strategies—be prepared to pivot quickly based on what's gaining traction among your target audience.

effectively utilizing Google Trends requires consistent engagement with its extensive dataset while remaining agile enough to adapt strategies accordingly. The more closely you monitor search behavior patterns using this tool, the better positioned you'll be not only to meet current user needs but also to anticipate future shifts within your industry landscape.

In summary, embracing the capabilities of Google Trends equips you with vital insights that enhance keyword selection and content creation strategies while enabling proactive engagement with evolving consumer interests—all essential components of successful SEO practices moving forward.

Creating a Keyword Strategy

Developing a robust keyword strategy is essential for effective SEO, closely linked to your broader content marketing initiatives. This process goes beyond merely identifying popular search terms; it involves creating a plan that aligns those keywords with user intent, competitive analysis, and your content creation process. A well-structured keyword strategy will not only inform your content but also clarify how to rank effectively in an increasingly crowded digital space.

To start, conduct a thorough analysis of your target audience. Understanding their needs, behaviors, and preferences is crucial for selecting the most relevant keywords. Take this example, if you're creating an online course for aspiring graphic designers, consider reaching out directly to potential students through surveys or social media discussions. This engagement can reveal the specific terms they use when searching for resources, leading to keyword choices that resonate with their actual queries.

Once you have insights into your audience, utilize tools like Ahrefs, SEMrush, or Moz to generate a comprehensive list of keywords. These platforms provide valuable metrics such as search volume, keyword difficulty, and related keywords. For example, when you input "graphic design courses," you may discover related phrases like "online graphic design certification" or "best graphic design schools." Each of these options carries different user intents and levels of competition. By analyzing these suggestions, you can expand your list and prioritize keywords that are both relevant and attainable in terms of ranking.

Incorporating long-tail keywords into your strategy is also important. These phrases are typically longer and more specific —think "affordable online graphic design courses for beginners." While they may have lower individual search volumes, their targeted nature often results in higher conversion rates since users searching for long-tail keywords typically have clearer intent. Crafting content around these terms can distinguish you from competitors who focus solely on broader keywords.

Organizing your keyword strategy with a clear hierarchy is essential for maintaining coherence. Establish primary keywords that represent overarching themes of your website, then categorize secondary and tertiary keywords beneath them. For example, if "graphic design" serves as your primary keyword, secondary keywords could include "graphic design tips" and "graphic design software." This hierarchy helps structure content across your site's pages and ensures each piece has a distinct purpose within the overall framework.

Evaluating competition for each keyword is another critical component. Conducting a competitive analysis enables you to identify who ranks for your target terms and the strategies they employ. Investigate the types of content they produce—are they using blog posts, videos, infographics? Tools like Ubersuggest can help you gauge the estimated traffic competitors receive from specific keywords. By understanding their successful approaches, you can create content that fills gaps in their offerings or presents information in a superior format.

Once you've chosen your keywords, implementing on-page SEO practices is vital for maximizing their effectiveness. Each page targeting specific keywords should have optimized title tags, meta descriptions, headers (H1s and H2s), and body content that naturally incorporates those terms. Take this example, if you're writing a blog post on "top graphic design trends," ensure the title tag clearly reflects this while offering value—perhaps "Top 10 Graphic Design Trends You Can't Miss in 2025." This clarity enhances search engine understanding and attracts clicks from users scanning search results.

Regularly revisiting and updating your keyword strategy is crucial for maintaining relevance over time. Market trends shift; new products emerge; consumer preferences evolve—and so should your focus areas. Set aside time quarterly to analyze performance data from Google Analytics or other tracking tools to identify which keywords are driving traffic and which may need reevaluation or replacement based on shifts in search patterns.

Finally, don't underestimate the importance of tracking user engagement metrics tied to your keyword strategy. Metrics such as click-through rates (CTR), bounce rates, and average session duration provide insights into how effectively users engage with content associated with specific keywords. If certain pages exhibit high bounce rates despite significant traffic numbers, it may indicate that users aren't finding what they expected upon clicking through—prompting you to refine not just the keyword focus but the overall user experience on those pages.

By crafting a dynamic keyword strategy grounded in audience understanding and adaptability to market trends, you'll position yourself ahead of competitors while providing genuine value to users seeking answers online. In today's ever-evolving SEO landscape—where algorithm changes can impact rankings overnight—an adaptable approach will empower you to remain responsive and effective in meeting both user needs and search engine expectations alike.

CHAPTER 4: ON-PAGE OPTIMIZATION STRATEGIES

The Importance of Content Quality

The importance of content quality in SEO is fundamental. It acts as the backbone of a successful strategy, directly impacting search rankings, user engagement, and brand credibility. High-quality content goes beyond simply presenting information; it focuses on delivering genuine value that meets the needs and expectations of your audience. This principle is at the heart of every effective SEO initiative and shapes all your marketing efforts.

To grasp why content quality is so crucial, consider how search engine algorithms are evolving. Google's frequent updates prioritize user experience, which means that content deemed relevant, informative, and engaging tends to rank higher. Take this example, if you manage a travel blog dedicated to budget-friendly destinations, creating comprehensive guides that cover affordable accommodations and local experiences not only addresses user queries but also increases dwell time on your site —an important metric for search engines.

Creating high-quality content starts with thorough research. Before writing, immerse yourself in your topic. Investigate trending discussions, analyze competitor articles, and consult reputable sources to gather insights that enrich your writing. If your focus is on "eco-friendly travel," for example, look into recent studies on sustainable tourism practices or share real-life stories of eco-conscious travelers. This depth not only enhances your content but also establishes you as an authority in your field.

Clarity in presentation is equally vital. Structure your content logically with clear headings and subheadings that guide readers through the material. Instead of grouping all information together, break down your article into easily digestible sections—such as introduction, main points, examples, and conclusion. This format improves readability and encourages users to spend more time on your page as they navigate well-defined sections.

Incorporating engaging storytelling can further elevate the quality of your content. Consider using anecdotes or case studies that resonate with your audience's experiences. For example, when discussing travel tips for backpackers, share a personal story from a memorable trip or include testimonials from fellow travelers. Stories forge emotional connections and can transform a straightforward article into a compelling narrative that captivates readers.

Multimedia elements also play a significant role in enhancing content quality. Including images, videos, infographics, or interactive features can greatly boost user engagement. Take this example, a blog post about healthy recipes might benefit from videos demonstrating cooking techniques or vibrant photos of finished dishes to visually entice viewers. This multimodal approach caters to diverse learning styles and can improve information retention.

After crafting high-quality content, ongoing optimization is essential for maintaining its effectiveness. Regularly update your pieces based on emerging trends or new data—this signals to both users and search engines that you are committed to providing fresh information. For example, if you manage a website focused on digital marketing trends, revisiting older posts to incorporate updated statistics or recent industry shifts showcases your authority and relevance in a rapidly changing field.

To evaluate the impact of your high-quality content on SEO performance, use analytics tools like Google Analytics or SEMrush to track metrics such as organic traffic growth and user engagement rates. Pay attention to which articles attract the most visitors or encourage prolonged interactions; this data can inform future content strategies.

Encouraging user interaction through comments and social media shares can amplify your content's reach and visibility. Foster discussions by posing questions at the end of articles or inviting readers to share their thoughts on social platforms. This two-way interaction not only boosts user engagement but also signals to search engines that your content resonates with audiences—potentially improving its ranking in search results.

content quality is not just a checkbox; it represents an ongoing commitment to delivering value and relevance in every piece you publish. By emphasizing research-driven insights, clear presentation, storytelling techniques, multimedia integration, continuous optimization efforts, analytical assessments, and fostering user interactions—you establish a solid foundation for successful SEO outcomes that enhance both visibility and trust within your target audience.

In today's competitive digital landscape where countless voices compete for attention, let the caliber of your content set you apart as a leader rather than just another contributor. This commitment will foster deeper connections with users while achieving significant SEO goals—an intersection where creativity meets strategic intent thrives at its finest.

Optimizing Headers (H1, H2, etc.)

Optimizing headers—particularly H1, H2, and other heading tags—is essential for effective on-page SEO. These elements not only organize your content but also significantly influence how search engines interpret and rank your web pages. By strategically using headers, you can enhance both user experience and search visibility.

The primary header, typically designated as H1, acts as the title of your page and should clearly convey its central theme. For example, if your content focuses on the benefits of meditation, an effective H1 could be "Unlocking Inner Peace: The Transformative Benefits of Meditation." This title is both direct and descriptive, providing immediate context for users and search engines alike.

Subheadings such as H2 and H3 further break down your content into manageable sections, improving readability. Organizing your content hierarchically—starting with broader concepts under H2s and delving into specific details with H3s—creates a clear path for readers to follow. Take this example, beneath the H2 "Health Benefits of Meditation," you could include multiple H3 subheadings like "Stress Reduction," "Improved Focus," and "Enhanced Emotional Well-Being." This logical structure not only aids user navigation but also signals to search engines the relative importance of different sections.

Incorporating keywords into your headers can strengthen your SEO efforts without resorting to keyword stuffing. Naturally weaving relevant keywords into headings helps signal content relevance to search engines while maintaining an organic feel for readers. When selecting keywords for your headers, consider using variations or synonyms that reflect user intent. For example, if you're targeting "mindfulness meditation," including it in an H2 like "Practicing Mindfulness Meditation for Daily Calm" effectively combines clarity with optimization.

Additionally, employing modifiers in your headers can enhance click-through rates from search engine results pages (SERPs). Words like "best," "top," or "ultimate" add specificity and resonate well with user queries. A good example would be changing "Benefits of Meditation" to "Top 7 Benefits of Meditation You Need to Know." This not only captures attention but also suggests that readers will gain actionable insights from your content.

Consistency in style and formatting across headers is also crucial. Whether you choose title case (capitalizing major words) or sentence case (capitalizing only the first word), maintaining a uniform approach enhances readability and gives your articles a polished appearance.

Implementing structured data through schema markup further enhances how search engines interpret headings on your page. By marking up headings appropriately—especially those framed as questions—you increase the potential to earn rich snippets in SERPs that showcase more engaging information than standard results. For example, a question like "What are the Benefits of Meditation?" tagged with suitable schema may appear as a featured snippet, boosting visibility significantly.

Engagement metrics provide invaluable insights into how well your header optimization resonates with users. Utilizing tools like Google Analytics or Ahrefs allows you to assess metrics such as average time on page or bounce rates after implementing header changes. If certain headlines result in increased engagement or lower bounce rates compared to others, they offer valuable evidence for refining future strategies.

optimizing headers isn't solely about improving rankings; it's about enhancing the experience for visitors who land on your pages. Headers guide users through their journey by clarifying what each section entails even before they dive into the text.

In summary, effective header optimization involves establishing a clear hierarchy through strategic use of H1s and subheadings while naturally integrating relevant keywords. This focus not only enhances user experience but also serves as a strong signal for search engines looking for high-quality content tailored to audience needs—ultimately positioning you favorably within competitive SERPs. Aim for headers that inform and entice; let them serve as bridges guiding readers deeper into engaging material rather than mere labels atop blocks of text.

Image Optimization Techniques

To begin with, choosing the right image format is crucial. JPEGs are ideal for photographs because they offer excellent compression without sacrificing quality. On the other hand, PNGs are better suited for images requiring transparency or intricate graphics. Meanwhile, WebP is a modern format that provides superior compression rates without any loss of quality, making it an excellent choice for web use. Take this example, converting a high-resolution JPEG image of 2 MB to WebP can reduce its size to under 500 KB, significantly improving page load times.

Next, consider image dimensions. Resizing images to match the exact display dimensions before uploading is essential. Uploading images larger than necessary can waste bandwidth and slow loading times. For example, if your website displays an image at 600x400 pixels, ensure the uploaded image is no larger than this size—preferably even smaller—to optimize loading efficiency.

Another key component often overlooked is alt text. Alt attributes serve multiple purposes: they provide context for search engines and improve accessibility for visually impaired users who rely on screen readers. When writing alt text, aim to be descriptive yet concise; a good rule of thumb is to keep it under 125 characters while incorporating relevant keywords where appropriate. For example, instead of using "image1234," describe it as "blue running shoes on a white background." This practice not only enhances relevance in search results but also makes your content more inclusive.

When naming your image files, a systematic approach can yield significant SEO benefits. Use clear and descriptive filenames rather than generic labels or random strings of numbers. Take this example, instead of naming an image "IMG_001," opt for "men-running-blue-shoes.jpg." This helps search engines understand the content better and contributes to improved indexing.

Implementing responsive images is another essential technique for optimizing visuals across various devices and screen sizes. Utilizing HTML attributes like "srcset" allows you to specify different versions of an image tailored to different resolutions or pixel densities. This guarantees that mobile users see appropriately sized images without compromising quality or speed—especially important as mobile search continues to dominate.

Additionally, image sitemaps can enhance visibility in search engines by explicitly informing them about your visual content. Including images in your sitemap ensures they're indexed properly, which can be particularly beneficial for websites with large catalogs or portfolios that heavily rely on visuals.

Lazy loading is another important aspect of image optimization. This technique defers the loading of off-screen images until they are about to enter the viewport, significantly improving initial load times and reducing overall server load. This creates a smoother experience for users navigating through pages filled with visuals.

Finally, don't underestimate the power of engaging visuals combined with user-generated content (UGC). Encouraging customers to share photos of themselves using your products not only enriches your site's imagery but also fosters community engagement and builds trust among potential buyers.

As you implement these image optimization techniques,

remember that each step contributes cumulatively to enhancing overall site performance and user experience. By treating every visual element with care—from selecting the right file format to ensuring optimal presentation across devices—you position your brand favorably in both users' eyes and search algorithms alike. Each optimized image acts as a digital ambassador for your brand, helping it stand out in a crowded digital landscape while ensuring effective communication across diverse platforms and audiences.

URL Structure Optimization

The first principle focuses on simplicity and clarity. A clean URL should clearly convey the topic of the page it represents. For example, "www.example.com/2025-seo-guide" is straightforward and descriptive, giving visitors a clear idea of what to expect. In contrast, a convoluted URL filled with multiple parameters or unrelated numbers can confuse both users and search engines alike. Aim for a URL structure that allows users to predict the content they'll find; this alignment fosters trust and encourages clicks.

In addition to clarity, incorporating relevant keywords into your URLs is vital for optimization. By integrating primary keywords that naturally reflect the main topic of your page, you help search engines categorize and rank your content more effectively. Take this example, if you operate an e-commerce site selling outdoor gear, a URL like "www.example.com/outdoor-backpacks" would likely perform better than "www.example.com/product123." However, be cautious of keyword stuffing—striking a balance is essential.

The length of your URLs also plays a significant role in their effectiveness. Search engines typically favor shorter URLs because they are easier to read and remember. While there's no strict rule regarding ideal length, keeping URLs under 60 characters is generally recommended. This length allows you to convey essential information while ensuring the links remain manageable for users who might want to share or bookmark them.

Another important consideration is the use of hyphens instead of underscores in your URLs. Hyphens serve as effective word separators for search engines, making it easier for them to parse individual terms within a URL. For example, "www.example.com/best-hiking-boots" is clearer than "www.example.com/best_hiking_boots." This seemingly small change can significantly influence how your content is indexed.

Maintaining a logical hierarchy within your URL structure is also beneficial for both usability and SEO. Organizing your site into categories and subcategories not only helps visitors navigate more intuitively but also provides context to search engines about the relationships between different pieces of content. Take this example, "www.example.com/outdoor/backpacks/mountain-backpacks" clearly indicates that mountain backpacks are a specific subset of outdoor gear.

Effectively utilizing canonical tags is another strategy to mitigate issues related to duplicate content. If you have similar content accessible via multiple URLs, implementing canonical tags informs search engines which version should be prioritized for indexing. This practice helps consolidate link equity and prevents splitting ranking signals across duplicates.

Additionally, redirects require careful attention during the URL optimization process. When changing URLs or removing pages, using 301 redirects ensures that both visitors and search engines are directed to the correct locations without losing traffic or rankings. Regularly auditing your site for broken links can further enhance user experience while safeguarding your SEO performance.

Finally, incorporating HTTPS into your URLs has transitioned from being optional to essential. Google increasingly favors secure sites in its ranking algorithms since HTTPS enhances user trust by protecting their data during interactions with your website. Although migrating from HTTP to HTTPS may involve some technical steps, the long-term benefits for SEO are significant.

As you refine your URL structure using these strategies, each adjustment contributes cumulatively to improved user engagement and search engine performance over time. Think of each optimized URL as a welcoming doorway into specific sections of your content; when these doors are easy to find, easy to understand, and secure, they not only attract traffic but also encourage visitors to explore further within your site's ecosystem—ultimately fostering brand loyalty and driving conversions.

Mobile-Friendly Web Design

At the heart of a mobile-friendly experience is responsive design. This approach ensures that your website seamlessly adapts to different screen sizes, making it accessible and visually appealing whether accessed via a smartphone, tablet, or desktop. One way to achieve this is through CSS media queries, which apply distinct styling rules based on the device's characteristics. For example:

```css
@media only screen and (max-width: 600px)
body
font-size: 14px;


.navigation
display: block;


```

This code snippet modifies the font size and navigation layout based on the screen width, thereby creating an optimized experience for users on smaller devices.

In addition to responsive design, loading speed is another critical factor for mobile sites. Research shows that users expect pages to load within two seconds; any delay can lead to increased bounce rates. To enhance load times on mobile, consider compressing images without sacrificing quality using tools like TinyPNG or ImageOptim. Employing responsive image tags can also serve appropriately sized images based on the device:

```html

Descriptive Alt Text

```

This HTML code enables browsers to select the most suitable image size according to screen resolution, thereby optimizing performance and improving user experience.

Touch-friendly navigation is equally important. Users should be able to interact with your site effortlessly using their fingers rather than requiring precise clicks. Design buttons with sufficient padding and space clickable elements adequately apart to avoid accidental clicks. Aim for buttons that are at least 44 pixels by 44 pixels; this recommendation aligns with Google's guidelines for touch targets.

For content layout on mobile platforms, careful consideration is essential. Prioritize content hierarchy by placing vital information above the fold—the portion of the page visible without scrolling. Utilize larger fonts and clear headings to guide users through your content effectively. A clean layout with ample white space not only enhances readability but also reduces cognitive load, making it easier for visitors to engage with your message.

It's important not to overlook the necessity of testing your mobile design across various devices and browsers. Tools like Google Mobile-Friendly Test can provide valuable insights into how well your site performs on mobile devices and identify areas needing improvement. Regular testing ensures that updates or changes do not compromise usability.

Integrating structured data can also enhance how search engines interpret your mobile content. Schema markup offers additional context about your pages, potentially leading to rich snippets that improve visibility in search results. Take this example, implementing local business schema can be especially beneficial for businesses targeting specific geographic areas:

```json

@context": "http://schema.org",
@type": "LocalBusiness",
name": "Your Business Name",
address":
@type": "PostalAddress",
streetAddress": "123 Main St",
addressLocality": "City",
addressRegion": "State",
postalCode": "12345

,
telephone": "+1-234-567-8901


```

By embedding this structured data into your HTML, you help search engines grasp essential details about your business location and services, thereby enhancing local search visibility.

Finally, monitoring user behavior through analytics tools offers insights into how visitors interact with your mobile site. Metrics such as bounce rates and average session durations can reveal how effectively your mobile design engages users. Use these insights to make iterative improvements tailored specifically to your audience's needs.

By implementing these strategies into your web design, you will significantly enhance both user experience and SEO performance as we move into this new era of digital engagement. Prioritizing responsiveness, loading speed, touch usability, content hierarchy, rigorous testing procedures, structured data implementation, and ongoing analytics monitoring will not only position you ahead of competitors but also foster a loyal audience eager to explore what you have to offer—regardless of their chosen device.

User Experience and Engagement

User experience (UX) and engagement have evolved from being mere supplementary aspects of SEO to becoming pivotal factors in determining search rankings and overall online success. As we approach 2025, search engines are increasingly prioritizing user satisfaction, making it essential for websites to not only attract traffic but also ensure that visitors remain engaged and satisfied once they arrive.

At the heart of effective user experience lies intuitive navigation. A well-structured website enables users to find what they need quickly and effortlessly. Think about the common frustrations users encounter—broken links, confusing menus, or excessive clicks required to access vital information. By simplifying navigation, you can significantly enhance user engagement. Implementing clear categories, a logical hierarchy, and a prominent search bar will help reduce bounce rates and encourage users to explore your site further.

Consider integrating breadcrumb navigation, which visually illustrates users' paths through your site. This technique improves usability while also benefiting SEO by creating additional internal links. For example, a breadcrumb structure might look like this:

Home > Category > Subcategory > Current Page

This setup allows users to backtrack easily if they want to explore related content without feeling lost or overwhelmed.

Loading speed is another critical factor in user engagement. Users have little tolerance for slow-loading pages—research shows that even a one-second delay can lead to significant drops in conversions. To address this, consider using techniques like lazy loading for images and videos. This approach ensures that content loads only when it enters the viewport, enhancing perceived performance by displaying initial content quickly while deferring less critical elements.

Here's an example of how you can implement lazy loading using JavaScript:

```javascript
document.addEventListener("DOMContentLoaded", function()

const lazyImages = document.querySelectorAll("img.lazy");

const options =

root: null,

rootMargin: "0px",

threshold: 0.1

;

const imageObserver = new IntersectionObserver((entries, observer) =>

entries.forEach(entry =>

if (entry.isIntersecting)

const img = entry.target;

img.src = img.dataset.src;

img.classList.remove("lazy");

observer.unobserve(img);
```

```
);
, options);
lazyImages.forEach(image =>
imageObserver.observe(image);
);
);
` ` `
```

This code snippet ensures that images tagged with the class "lazy" are only loaded as they come into view, helping to achieve faster initial page load times.

However, engagement goes beyond speed and navigation; the quality of your content is equally vital. Reflect on how your content resonates with your audience's needs and interests. Crafting engaging material requires an understanding of user intent—what visitors are truly searching for when they arrive on your page. Using storytelling techniques, such as case studies or relatable narratives, can create emotional connections with readers and foster deeper engagement.

Incorporating interactive elements like polls, quizzes, or infographics can transform passive readers into active participants on your site. These features not only extend the time users spend on your pages but also encourage social sharing—a crucial factor in building authority and backlinks.

Mobile optimization is another essential component of enhancing user experience. With over half of internet traffic originating from mobile devices, a responsive design must prioritize touch interaction and readability across various screen sizes. Ensuring buttons are appropriately sized for touch interaction will help prevent frustration; following Google's recommendations for button sizes—at least 44 pixels by 44 pixels—will improve the experience for mobile users who may struggle with precise clicks on smaller screens.

Tracking user interactions through analytics tools can provide insights into how effectively your design engages visitors. Metrics such as time spent on page and click-through rates offer actionable insights into areas needing improvement. Take this example, high bounce rates on specific pages may indicate that the content fails to meet visitor expectations or that the layout does not entice further exploration.

Incorporating feedback mechanisms such as surveys or comment sections invites direct communication from users about their experiences on your site. This feedback loop allows you to refine your approach based on actual visitor behavior rather than assumptions.

Lastly, integrating structured data can enhance how search engines interpret your content's relevance while improving visibility in SERPs through rich snippets. This structured approach facilitates better indexing while conveying vital information about your services directly in search results—a win-win for both SEO performance and user satisfaction.

Prioritizing user experience is no longer optional; it's essential for successful SEO strategies in 2025 and beyond. By focusing on intuitive navigation, fast loading speeds, quality engagement-driven content, mobile optimization strategies, analytics monitoring, direct feedback collection methods, and structured data implementations, you not only enhance user satisfaction but also significantly improve your website's potential ranking across search engines.

As you work on improving UX within your SEO strategies today, remember that every small adjustment contributes to building a stronger relationship with your audience—a partnership grounded in trust that encourages them to return again and again.

Implementation of Schema Markup

Implementing schema markup is a vital strategy for enhancing your SEO efforts, especially as search engines become increasingly adept at interpreting web content. Schema markup, a type of microdata, helps search engines better understand the context of your content, which can significantly improve how your pages appear in search results. As we look ahead to 2025, mastering this technique will be crucial for distinguishing yourself from a crowded field of competitors.

To begin, it's important to familiarize yourself with the different types of schema markup and their specific applications. For example, if you own a local business, utilizing LocalBusiness schema allows you to clearly communicate essential information such as your business name, address, and hours of operation. Alternatively, if you manage a blog featuring articles or reviews, implementing Article schema can enhance the visibility of your posts with rich snippets that display star ratings and publication dates.

Getting started with schema markup is straightforward, thanks to tools like Google's Structured Data Markup Helper. This user-friendly tool enables you to create the necessary code by tagging elements directly on your webpage. Take this example, if you want to mark up a recipe on your food blog, you would select the "Recipe" type and begin tagging elements like the recipe title, ingredients, cooking time, and nutritional information. Here's a step-by-step guide on how to do this:

1. Go to the Structured Data Markup Helper.

2. Choose "Recipe" from the list of data types.

3. Enter your webpage URL or paste your HTML code into the tool.

4. Tag each relevant section—such as title, ingredients, and instructions—with the appropriate markup.

5. Generate the code and incorporate it into your

webpage's HTML.

Once you've implemented schema markup, validating it is essential to ensure everything is correctly formatted and functioning as intended. You can use Google's Rich Results Test tool to verify whether your markup qualifies for rich results in search engines. Simply input your URL or paste in the generated code; any errors will be highlighted for correction.

In addition to enriching your content with more information, structured data plays another important role: enhancing visibility through rich snippets. These additional details in search results make your listings more informative at first glance. Take this example, when users see review stars next to a product or article title in SERPs, they are more likely to click through due to the perceived credibility and value.

Consider a local bakery that implements schema markup for its offerings. By marking up their menu items with Product schema—complete with price ranges and availability—they can improve their ranking potential while attracting users specifically searching for bakery goods in their area.

And, as you utilize existing schemas from Schema.org—a collaborative initiative supported by major search engines—stay alert for new types that may emerge as technology advances. Take this example, with the rise of augmented reality (AR) in e-commerce experiences, related schemas may be introduced that enable businesses to showcase AR features directly in search results.

Keeping abreast of these developments is crucial. Regularly revisiting your structured data implementation allows you to take advantage of new features that could further enhance visibility or user engagement.

After applying schema markup, monitoring performance can provide valuable insights into its impact on your SEO efforts. Tools like Google Analytics and Google Search Console can help you track metrics such as click-through rates (CTR) and impressions associated with pages featuring structured data versus those without it.

Incorporating user feedback is also essential; if specific content performs exceptionally well after implementing schema markup while other content struggles, examining those discrepancies can help refine your future strategies.

While structured data is beneficial for improving visibility and engagement within SERPs, it's important to remember that it is not a catch-all solution for SEO challenges. Instead, it serves as one component of a broader strategy aimed at enhancing overall user experience and satisfaction.

As we approach 2025, effectively integrating schema markup will not only increase your site's chances of ranking higher but also foster greater user engagement through richer interactions within search results—an increasingly vital aspect in today's competitive landscape.

By focusing on understanding various available schemas today, rigorously validating them after application, and monitoring their performance, you are setting yourself up for success in mastering this indispensable element of modern SEO practice. This will ensure that you keep pace with evolving algorithms while effectively meeting user expectations head-on.

Page Load Speed Optimization

Page load speed is more than a mere technical metric; it is a vital element that directly affects user experience and search engine optimization (SEO) rankings. As online users grow increasingly impatient, even a delay of just a few seconds can lead to significant drops in traffic and conversions. By 2025, optimizing page load speed will be essential for anyone aiming to enhance their online presence and maintain a competitive edge.

To begin the optimization process, assess your current performance using tools like Google PageSpeed Insights,

GTmetrix, and Pingdom. These resources provide valuable insights into how quickly your pages load and highlight areas for improvement. For example, if you operate an e-commerce site selling shoes, you may discover that product pages with high-resolution images are taking too long to load. Identifying this bottleneck is crucial for addressing it effectively.

Once you have established baseline data, the next step is to minimize HTTP requests. Each element on your webpage—such as images, scripts, and stylesheets—requires a separate request from the server. Simplifying your design can significantly reduce these requests. Consider consolidating CSS files or utilizing CSS sprites to combine multiple images into one file. This approach not only cuts down on the number of requests but also streamlines the rendering process.

Another important aspect of improving load speed is optimizing images without compromising quality. Tools like TinyPNG or ImageOptim can effectively compress images. Take this example, if your site features a gallery of shoe images, reducing their file sizes while maintaining clarity will lead to faster loading times. Additionally, using next-gen formats such as WebP instead of JPEG or PNG can further enhance performance due to their smaller file sizes.

Implementing lazy loading is another effective strategy to consider. This technique defers the loading of non-essential resources until they are needed—typically when they enter the viewport. For example, in your shoe store, product images can load as users scroll down the page rather than all at once. This approach significantly reduces initial loading time and enhances the overall user experience.

Content Delivery Networks (CDNs) also play a crucial role in speeding up website access by distributing content across various servers worldwide. When a user visits your site, the CDN delivers content from the nearest server location, which drastically reduces latency. Setting up a CDN for your shoe store ensures that customers accessing your site from different geographical locations enjoy faster load times.

Minifying CSS, JavaScript, and HTML files is another effective method for enhancing speed. By removing unnecessary characters such as whitespace and comments from code, you reduce file sizes and improve loading times. Tools like UglifyJS for JavaScript or CSSNano for CSS can help automate this process.

And, ensuring that your website is mobile-friendly directly impacts load speed since mobile users often experience slower connections compared to desktop users. Google's Mobile-Friendly Test tool can identify issues specific to mobile devices. If a large percentage of traffic to your shoe store comes from mobile users, ensuring fast load times on these platforms is crucial.

Browser caching is another tactic worth considering; it allows frequently accessed resources to be stored locally in users' browsers so they don't need to reload each time they visit your site. Implementing proper cache control headers ensures that returning visitors experience quicker loading times.

Lastly, conducting regular audits of your website's performance with tools mentioned earlier will help you stay informed about any new issues that may arise due to changes in content or technology standards.

Take this example, after implementing these strategies in your e-commerce shoe store, you might see improvements in page speed scores in Google PageSpeed Insights—from 65% to 85%. Such enhancements could lead to higher user retention rates and improved conversion metrics over time.

To wrap things up, prioritizing page load speed optimization goes beyond mere technical adjustments; it's about enriching user experience and remaining relevant in an ever-evolving digital landscape. As we approach 2025, businesses that actively focus on these improvements are likely to reap substantial rewards through increased traffic and customer satisfaction—ultimately paving the way for sustained success online.

CHAPTER 5:
TECHNICAL SEO
MASTERY

Understanding Site Architecture

Understanding your website's structure is essential for effective SEO. Site architecture refers to how content is organized, categorized, and interlinked. A well-structured site not only enhances user experience but also facilitates search engine crawling and indexing, which directly influences your visibility in search results. As we approach 2025, mastering site architecture has never been more critical.

Visualize your site as a tree, with a strong trunk and sprawling branches. The trunk symbolizes your homepage—where every user should begin their journey. From this central point, you branch out into categories that house related content, creating a logical flow that guides visitors deeper into your site. For example, if you run a blog about healthy living, the trunk might lead to branches like "Nutrition," "Exercise," and "Mental Well-being." Each of these branches should link to relevant subtopics that enhance user engagement and encourage exploration.

When building this architecture, pay close attention to your

URL structure. Clean, descriptive URLs are easier for both users and search engines to comprehend. Instead of using long strings of numbers or irrelevant words like www.example.com/category/12345?=xyz, opt for something intuitive like www.example.com/nutrition/healthy-recipes. This approach not only aids in SEO but also improves click-through rates by providing users with a clear indication of the content ahead.

Next, concentrate on internal linking strategies. Every link on your site serves as a pathway that connects visitors from one page to another while helping search engines navigate effectively. By strategically placing links within your content —such as referencing related articles or popular posts—you enhance navigation and distribute page authority throughout your site. Take this example, if you have an article discussing the benefits of meditation under "Mental Well-being," consider linking to other relevant resources that explore specific techniques or personal success stories.

Hierarchy is another crucial aspect to consider. Use header tags (H1, H2, H3) thoughtfully to establish a clear content hierarchy. Your homepage should typically contain one H1 tag that encapsulates its main theme—something like "Healthy Living Made Easy." From there, subtopics can utilize H2 tags (e.g., "Nutrition Tips") to break down information into digestible segments that are easy for both users and search engines to navigate.

Additionally, breadcrumb navigation can significantly enhance user experience and improve SEO performance. Breadcrumbs provide users with a visual trail that indicates their location within the website's hierarchy—acting as a digital map. For example: Home > Mental Well-being > Benefits of Meditation allows users to easily backtrack if they wish to explore other topics without repeatedly hitting the back button.

Accessibility is also pivotal in site architecture; it ensures that all users can navigate seamlessly, regardless of their device or ability level. Implementing responsive design techniques guarantees that your layout adapts across various devices while maintaining usability—especially crucial as mobile searches continue to rise.

Another closely related factor is load speed; how quickly pages render can significantly impact bounce rates. If users encounter delays while navigating through complex hierarchies or poorly optimized structures, they may abandon their search entirely—a lost opportunity for engagement and conversion.

Regular audits can help assess how well your architecture aligns with current SEO practices. Tools like Screaming Frog or Sitebulb can identify broken links or problematic navigation paths that need addressing.

Take this example, if you're revamping an existing e-commerce website focused on eco-friendly products, reviewing its architecture might reveal disorganized categories with overlapping products leading to shopper confusion. Streamlining categories such as "Reusable Bags" and "Eco-Friendly Kitchenware" into distinct sections creates clarity and boosts internal linking opportunities, enabling customers to find what they need without feeling overwhelmed.

Investing time in developing robust site architecture lays the groundwork for SEO success as we move into 2025 and beyond. An intuitive structure promotes user engagement while enhancing search engine visibility—a dual advantage in today's competitive landscape where every click counts toward driving traffic and conversions on digital platforms.

The Role of XML Sitemaps

XML sitemaps are crucial in the intricate realm of SEO, serving as essential roadmaps that help search engines understand and navigate your website's structure. Imagine an XML sitemap as a comprehensive index that not only lists your site's pages but also illustrates their relationships and relative importance. This clarity significantly enhances how effectively search engines like Google can crawl, index, and rank your content. As you refine your SEO strategies for 2025, mastering the creation and management of XML sitemaps will be vital.

While creating an XML sitemap may seem intimidating at first, the process becomes straightforward when broken down into manageable steps. Many content management systems (CMS) provide plugins or built-in features for automatic sitemap generation. For example, if you're using WordPress, popular plugins like Yoast SEO or Rank Math can automatically generate and update your XML sitemap without requiring any technical expertise. Once activated, these plugins create a URL such as www.example.com/sitemap.xml, which serves as a gateway for search engines to access all the essential pages on your site.

However, simply generating a sitemap is not sufficient. It's important to ensure that it remains accurate and reflective of your current site structure. Regular updates are necessary whenever you add new content or make significant changes to existing pages; an outdated sitemap could hinder search engine bots from discovering fresh material, leading to missed opportunities for indexing and ranking.

When structuring your XML sitemap, focus on including only high-quality pages that provide value. This means excluding duplicate content or low-value pages that might dilute your site's overall quality in the eyes of search engines. Take this example, if several blog posts cover similar topics, consider consolidating them into a single comprehensive resource instead of listing each individual post separately in your sitemap.

Incorporating additional information within your XML sitemap —such as last modified dates and priority levels for individual pages—is also beneficial. Specifying when a page was last updated signals to search engines which content is most relevant and should be crawled more frequently. Setting priority levels helps indicate which pages are most important; while this doesn't directly affect rankings, it guides search engines on where to focus their crawling efforts first.

For smaller websites, managing sitemaps manually can be effective. However, larger sites often require more sophisticated approaches due to their scale and complexity. In these cases, tools like Screaming Frog can help visualize how different sections of your site are connected and identify potential issues with page links or structures before they become problematic during crawls.

Additionally, submitting your XML sitemap to Google Search Console is crucial for optimizing visibility in search results. Once submitted through the 'Sitemaps' section of Search Console, you'll receive notifications about indexing status or any errors encountered by Google's crawlers—providing essential feedback that allows you to continuously refine both the sitemap itself and your overall SEO strategies.

For example, consider an e-commerce website specializing in handmade crafts with thousands of products categorized by type (such as jewelry or home décor). To optimize visibility effectively, create separate XML sitemaps for each category rather than cramming all URLs into one lengthy document. By submitting multiple sitemaps categorized by section (e.g., www.example.com/sitemap-jewelry.xml), you streamline navigation for crawlers while ensuring they can quickly locate all relevant product listings.

And, integrating multimedia elements—such as video or image URLs—into XML sitemaps enriches user engagement across diverse platforms. Utilizing media-specific extensions allows video thumbnails or alternate formats to appear prominently in search results—a critical factor in capturing user attention in an increasingly visual online landscape.

developing a robust strategy around XML sitemaps requires a commitment to continuous improvement in line with evolving trends in user behavior and technological advancements within the SEO landscape. By treating sitemaps not merely as static documents but as dynamic tools integral to enhancing overall digital marketing strategies, marketers can position themselves favorably in competitive environments where precision matters immensely.

Investing time in mastering XML sitemaps provides businesses with powerful leverage over their search engine presence moving forward—an indispensable component for achieving lasting success online as we approach 2025 and beyond.

Robots.txt and Its Best Practices

The robots.txt file is essential for guiding search engines as they navigate your website. Acting as a set of instructions, this file informs search engine crawlers about which pages to explore and which to avoid. Located at the root of your domain (for example, www.example.com/robots.txt), crafting an effective robots.txt file is crucial for managing the flow of search engine traffic. It helps ensure that your most valuable content receives the attention it deserves while shielding less important areas from unnecessary crawling.

To effectively utilize the robots.txt file, it's important to understand its syntax and structure. The file comprises directives, primarily "User-agent" and "Disallow." The "User-agent" directive specifies which crawler the rules apply to, whereas "Disallow" indicates specific pages or sections that should not be crawled. Take this example, if you wish to prevent all crawlers from accessing an admin panel, your robots.txt would look like this:

```
` ` `

User-agent: *
Disallow: /admin/

` ` `
```

This simple directive instructs all user agents (crawlers) not to index anything within the /admin/ directory. On the other hand, if there are areas you want all crawlers to access, you can use the "Allow" directive. This is particularly useful when a parent directory is disallowed but specific files or subdirectories need to remain accessible.

Consider a website with a general disallow rule for its development environment but still wants search engines to crawl its homepage:

```
` ` `

User-agent: *

Disallow: /dev/

Allow: /dev/index.html

` ` `
```

In this scenario, crawlers are blocked from accessing everything in the /dev/ directory except for index.html, ensuring that while your development site stays private, users can still discover the essential landing page.

Using robots.txt also offers opportunities for optimization; however, it's important not to overuse disallow directives indiscriminately. Blocking critical pages or sections can lead to missed indexing opportunities and negatively impact your rankings. A common mistake is preventing crawlers from indexing JavaScript or CSS files that are vital for rendering pages correctly. If search engines cannot access these resources, it may result in poor user experience assessments and lower rankings.

Before deploying your robots.txt file live, testing it can save you potential headaches down the line. Google Search Console features a Robots Testing Tool that allows you to input your rules and verify their functionality. After making changes, consistently monitor Google Search Console for any crawl errors related to the directives in your robots.txt file.

To illustrate best practices in action, consider an online retailer that launches seasonal promotions but wishes to prevent crawlers from accessing outdated promotional pages after their expiration. By adding rules like the following to their robots.txt:

` ` `

User-agent: *

Disallow: /promotions/expired/

` ` `

The retailer effectively safeguards outdated content while ensuring that active promotional pages remain visible for discovery by search engines.

However, it's crucial to remember that while robots.txt is powerful, it is not a foolproof security mechanism. Sensitive information should be secured through proper authentication methods rather than solely relying on disallowing crawls; anyone could still manually visit those URLs if they know them.

Utilizing additional tools can deepen your understanding of how robots interact with your site. By combining insights from web analytics platforms—such as monitoring referral traffic—you can assess whether blocking certain areas impacts overall visibility or engagement metrics.

As we look ahead to 2025 and beyond, adopting a proactive approach toward your robots.txt strategy will provide a competitive advantage. Regularly revisiting and refining this crucial component ensures alignment with evolving SEO practices while maximizing crawl efficiency and protecting sensitive areas of your website.

By viewing the robots.txt file not merely as a technical necessity but as an integral part of your broader SEO strategy, you can position yourself favorably against competitors who may overlook its importance. This proactive stance ultimately paves the way for enhanced search visibility and improved user engagement in an ever-evolving digital landscape.

Advanced Canonicalization Techniques

A foundational element of canonicalization is the effective use of the rel="canonical" tag. When implemented correctly, this tag signals to search engines that a specific page is the authoritative source for a piece of content. For example, if you run an e-commerce website selling shoes and have several URLs for the same product due to various filters or parameters (like color or size), using a canonical tag can help consolidate these variations into one preferred URL. This approach simplifies your site's structure and directs all ranking signals to that single URL, thereby boosting its visibility in search results.

Consider a product page with different URLs like:

- www.example.com/shoes?color=red

- www.example.com/shoes?color=blue

- www.example.com/shoes?size=10

In this scenario, you would implement a canonical tag in each variant pointing to the primary version: www.example.com/shoes. This strategy not only helps avoid potential duplicate content penalties but also enhances user experience by guiding visitors to the most relevant page.

Another important technique involves effectively managing URL parameters. These parameters often arise from tracking tools or filter options on e-commerce sites. While they can provide valuable data for analysis, they may also create multiple versions of similar pages that confuse search engines. Utilizing Google Search Console allows you to specify how Google should handle these parameters—whether it should crawl them or ignore them entirely. Proper configuration ensures that only essential variations are indexed while maintaining the integrity of your site's SEO strategy.

If your site targets users across different languages or regions, consider implementing hreflang attributes. This is especially beneficial for global brands with multilingual websites where similar content exists in various language versions. Take this example, if you have both English and Spanish versions of your site, using hreflang tags informs search engines which audience each page serves. An implementation might look like this:

```html

```

This practice ensures that users see content tailored to their language preferences, enhancing engagement and retention while avoiding unnecessary duplication issues.

Redirects also play a crucial role in advanced canonicalization strategies. When redirecting old URLs to new ones—such as during a site redesign or when merging content—it's essential to use 301 redirects instead of temporary 302 redirects. A 301 redirect transfers about 90-99% of link equity from the old URL to the new one, helping preserve its rankings and relevance.

However, it's important to be cautious with redirect chains; excessive chaining can dilute link equity and slow down page load times, negatively impacting user experience and SEO performance. Instead of creating long redirect paths (e.g., A -> B -> C), aim for direct redirects from A -> C whenever possible.

Regular audits of your website's canonical tags are also essential. Tools like Screaming Frog or Ahrefs can help identify potential issues with duplicate content or incorrect implementations of canonical tags. These tools provide insights into how search engines perceive your site's structure and highlight areas that may need improvement.

As algorithms continue to evolve with an emphasis on user experience and relevance, mastering advanced canonicalization techniques is crucial for any serious SEO professional. By clearly defining preferred URLs through strategic tagging and management practices, you're not just optimizing for search engines; you're also enhancing the overall experience for users navigating your site.

Embracing these advanced strategies empowers you to take

control over how your content is perceived in an increasingly complex digital landscape. The nuances involved in effective canonicalization will significantly contribute to your site's authority and visibility online—key components in achieving long-term SEO success.

Fixing Crawl Errors

Crawl errors can be the silent saboteurs of your SEO efforts, quietly undermining your website's performance. These errors arise when search engine bots attempt to access your site but encounter obstacles, preventing effective indexing of your pages. Addressing these issues goes beyond appeasing algorithms; it's essential for fostering a seamless user experience and upholding your site's credibility.

The first step in resolving crawl errors is identification. Google Search Console is an invaluable resource for this task. By navigating to the "Coverage" report, you can uncover various types of errors, including 404s (Page Not Found), server errors, and soft 404s (where a page returns a success status while displaying an error message). Each type requires a tailored approach.

Take the common 404 error, for example. Picture a scenario where users click on a link to a product page that no longer exists. This frustrating experience can lead to higher bounce rates and erode trust in your brand. To remedy this, set up 301 redirects for any deleted pages that previously had inbound links or were indexed. This approach informs both search engines and visitors that the content has permanently moved to a new location. Take this example, if your old page was:

www.example.com/old-product,

and you've created an updated product page at:

www.example.com/new-product,

implementing a 301 redirect ensures a smooth transition of traffic, preserving user engagement and SEO value.

Another common issue is server errors (5xx errors), which signal problems on the server side that prevent pages from loading. When search engines encounter these errors, they may remove your pages from their index entirely. If you experience a 500 Internal Server Error, consult server logs to diagnose the issue—whether it stems from scripts timing out or excessive memory usage—and collaborate with your hosting provider for a swift resolution. Frequent outages can convey instability to search engines, negatively affecting your rankings over time.

In addition to addressing individual errors, maintaining an ongoing audit strategy is crucial. Tools like Screaming Frog or Ahrefs can help you crawl your site regularly. These tools not only identify current crawl errors but also provide insights into potential technical issues that could hinder performance in the future.

Take this example, discovering numerous broken internal links during an audit may indicate poor site management or outdated content structures. Fixing these broken links is not just housekeeping; it strengthens your internal linking strategy and helps distribute link equity more effectively throughout your site.

Additionally, pay attention to how search engines interpret URL parameters on your pages. These parameters can create multiple variations of the same content, leading to duplicate content issues if not managed correctly. Within Google Search Console's settings under "URL Parameters," you can specify how Google should treat these variations—whether they should be crawled or ignored entirely.

Regularly updating and maintaining a clean sitemap is another proactive step in preventing crawl errors from becoming problematic. Submitting an updated XML sitemap through Google Search Console allows search engines to promptly discover new content while highlighting any discrepancies between what you want indexed and what is currently being crawled.

Lastly, staying informed about evolving best practices in SEO and crawl error management is essential. The digital landscape is ever-changing; strategies that worked yesterday may not be effective today. Engaging with industry experts through webinars or forums can offer fresh perspectives on tackling common challenges.

To wrap things up, fixing crawl errors requires diligence and strategic intervention. It's not merely about correcting problems; it's about creating an optimized environment where users can navigate smoothly while search engines efficiently index your content. By prioritizing these efforts, you enhance both user experience and search visibility—two critical components for achieving long-term success in your SEO initiatives.

Secure and Accessible Websites (HTTPS)

Shifting our focus from crawl errors to the security and accessibility of your website uncovers a crucial dimension of SEO strategy. While it is essential to resolve issues that hinder search engines from crawling your site, securing your website with HTTPS encryption is equally important for fostering user trust and enhancing search engine rankings.

The transition to HTTPS has become standard in web development, largely due to growing concerns about data security and privacy. By 2025, consumers are expected to be more discerning about their online interactions, viewing security as a baseline requirement rather than an optional feature. When users notice the padlock icon in their browser's address bar, it signals that their data is encrypted, which builds trust and encourages them to engage with your site. In contrast, websites still operating on HTTP may deter visitors who perceive potential risks, pushing them towards competitors that prioritize security.

Implementing HTTPS begins with obtaining an SSL (Secure

Socket Layer) certificate. This process starts by selecting a reputable Certificate Authority (CA). You can choose from well-known providers like Let's Encrypt, which offers free certificates, or opt for paid services that come with added features such as warranty and support. After acquiring the certificate, installation is typically straightforward; many hosting providers offer one-click installations for SSL certificates, simplifying the setup process significantly.

Once your SSL certificate is installed, it's essential to ensure that all elements of your site—scripts, images, stylesheets—are also served over HTTPS. Failing to do so can result in mixed content warnings when secure pages link to unsecured resources, which may negatively impact user experience and SEO performance. Use your browser's developer tools to identify any mixed content issues. For example, if your homepage includes images served via HTTP while the rest of the content is on HTTPS, browsers might block those images from loading altogether.

After migrating to HTTPS, updating any internal links throughout your site is critical. Look for hardcoded URLs pointing to HTTP versions of your pages and change them to HTTPS. This guarantees seamless navigation and maintains your site's link equity. Conducting a comprehensive audit using tools like Screaming Frog or SEMrush can help you identify these discrepancies efficiently.

Incorporating 301 redirects from HTTP to HTTPS should also be part of your strategy. This action not only informs search engines that a page has permanently moved to a new secure location but also preserves valuable link equity built over time. Neglecting proper redirects can lead search engines to treat the HTTP and HTTPS versions as separate entities, potentially splitting traffic and harming your rankings.

Beyond these technical measures, it's important to consider how HTTPS influences user behavior on your site. Enhanced security features can lead to higher conversion rates; research by Google indicates that sites using HTTPS experience improved engagement metrics. Customers are more inclined to complete transactions on secure platforms because they feel safer sharing sensitive information.

Accessibility plays an equally vital role in SEO performance under HTTPS protocols. As you bolster site security, ensure compliance with accessibility standards (such as WCAG) so all users—including those with disabilities—can navigate your website without difficulty. This approach not only expands your audience but also aligns with ethical web design best practices.

As technology continues to advance, search engines increasingly favor secure websites in their ranking algorithms. By 2025, neglecting this standard could result in reduced visibility in search results as competitors who prioritize security gain prominence.

In summary, transitioning to HTTPS not only protects user data but also serves as a foundational element of modern SEO strategy. By securing your website through an SSL certificate and adhering to best practices for web security and accessibility, you cultivate a trustworthy digital presence that appeals to both users and search engines alike. Investing in security today translates into enhanced user retention and improved rankings tomorrow—an essential insight for any serious SEO practitioner aiming for excellence in the digital landscape.

Handling Domain Migrations

Navigating the intricate landscape of domain migrations is a vital skill for any SEO professional. Whether you're changing your domain for branding purposes, consolidating multiple sites, or transitioning from a subdomain to a root domain, managing these migrations effectively can have a profound impact on your search visibility and user experience. A well-planned migration not only protects your hard-earned rankings but also enhances the overall effectiveness of your online presence.

The first step in any successful domain migration is thorough planning. Begin by auditing your current site to document all URLs, content, and backlinks. Tools such as Screaming Frog or Ahrefs can help generate a comprehensive list of existing pages along with their corresponding metrics. This data is essential, serving as a reference point to ensure that no valuable traffic is lost during the transition. For example, if your existing site has 200 pages indexed in Google, it's crucial to ensure that each one has a corresponding page on the new domain.

Once you have gathered this information, consider how the new domain aligns with your brand strategy. Selecting a new domain name involves more than simply finding an available URL; it should embody your business ethos and be memorable for users. If you're rebranding or modifying your service offerings, it's important that the new domain resonates with both current and prospective customers. To gauge public perception, consider conducting surveys or soliciting feedback on potential names.

After choosing a new domain and mapping out your URL structure, it's time to address the technical aspects of the migration. Implement 301 redirects from old URLs to their new counterparts. This step is critical as it informs search engines that content has permanently moved, helping to preserve link equity and minimize disruptions in traffic flow. Take this example, if you're transitioning from www.oldwebsite.com/page1 to www.newwebsite.com/page1, the redirect ensures that any traffic directed to the old page seamlessly flows to the new one.

Monitoring these redirects after the migration is just as important as setting them up. Utilize tools like Google Search Console to identify crawl errors or broken links that may arise from misconfigured redirects. If users encounter 404 error pages after the migration—a common pitfall—you risk losing potential customers and undermining trust in your brand.

In addition to technical adjustments, it's crucial to

communicate with stakeholders about the upcoming changes. Informing customers through email newsletters or social media can help alleviate concerns about any potential disruptions during the transition. Emphasizing benefits such as improved site speed or an enhanced user experience can further mitigate apprehensions associated with change.

Another important aspect is updating external links that point to your old domain. Reach out to partners and websites that link back to you, requesting updates where applicable. This outreach not only strengthens relationships but also ensures that valuable backlinks continue directing traffic to your new site.

During this transition period, closely monitor analytics data to gain insights into user behavior before and after the migration. Tools like Google Analytics or Matomo can help track traffic patterns and key metrics such as bounce rates and average session duration; significant changes may indicate issues with user interaction on the newly migrated site.

As you settle into the post-migration phase, continuously assess search rankings for important keywords associated with your business. It's common for rankings to fluctuate initially after a migration due to re-indexing by search engines; however, monitoring these changes will provide valuable insights into how well the migration has been executed.

In addition to tracking keyword performance, evaluate visitor engagement with your content on the new domain compared to before. This analysis should include conversion rates as well as general user feedback regarding navigation and accessibility features. Positive responses can reinforce that you're on the right track, while negative feedback will highlight areas that need attention.

A successful domain migration demands meticulous attention throughout every phase—from planning through execution and post-launch assessment. Each step plays an integral role in maintaining SEO health and preserving brand integrity during times of change.

executing a thoughtful domain migration not only safeguards existing traffic but can also rejuvenate interest in your brand by creating fresh engagement opportunities in search results—reminding everyone why they valued you in the first place while setting the stage for future growth.

The Impact of Structured Data

Structured data, commonly known as schema markup, has become an essential tool in the SEO toolkit. Its importance lies in its ability to improve how search engines interpret content, providing clearer context and understanding. By implementing structured data, you can significantly enhance how your site appears in search results, potentially increasing click-through rates (CTR) and boosting overall visibility.

At its essence, structured data offers a standardized format for describing a webpage and categorizing its content. For example, by utilizing the schema.org vocabulary, you can inform search engines that a specific piece of content is an article, a recipe, or a product. This clarity allows Google to deliver more relevant results to users searching for related topics.

Take, for instance, the application of structured data on a local business website. By marking up vital information—such as the business name, address, phone number, and operating hours—with LocalBusiness schema markup, you improve your chances of appearing in local search results enriched with rich snippets. These snippets display crucial information directly in search results, making it easier for potential customers to engage with your business without needing to visit your website first.

To begin integrating structured data into your site, start by identifying which elements of your content could benefit from markup. Google offers tools like the Structured Data Markup Helper to assist you in creating appropriate markup for various content types. After generating your markup code—usually in

JSON-LD format—you'll need to incorporate it into the HTML of your web pages. If you're not using a plugin that simplifies this process, access to your CMS or HTML files may be necessary.

For example, if you operate an online bookstore and wish to enhance your product pages with structured data, you could implement Product schema to specify details such as the book title, author name, ISBN number, price, and availability status. This approach means that when someone searches for "buy [Book Title] online," Google may display not only a link but also rich snippets showcasing the book's price and ratings directly in the search results.

After adding structured data to your site, validating its implementation is crucial. Utilize Google's Rich Results Test tool or Schema Markup Validator to check for errors in your markup. Errors can hinder search engines from accurately interpreting your structured data; therefore, this validation step is essential before going live.

Once validated and implemented correctly on live pages, keep an eye on how these changes impact performance through Google Search Console. The performance report will reveal if any new rich results appear and how they influence user engagement metrics—such as CTR and average position—in organic search results.

Understanding user behavior is vital; analyzing which types of rich snippets drive more traffic can guide future optimization efforts. If certain products garner significant clicks due to their enhanced presentation on SERPs through structured data markup, consider extending similar enhancements across other product lines or different content types on your site.

It's important to note that while structured data greatly improves visibility in search results, it does not guarantee higher rankings outright. Instead, it serves as an additional layer of context that helps search engines better understand and serve your content based on user intent and relevance.

As voice search grows increasingly popular with smart speakers and mobile assistants, structured data becomes even more critical in ensuring accurate responses from these technologies. By marking up FAQs or relevant queries on your website using appropriate schemas like FAQPage or QAPage markup, you prepare yourself for evolving trends where traditional keyword searches transition into conversational inquiries.

Lastly, staying informed about evolving guidelines regarding structured data is essential as search engine algorithms continually adapt. Regularly reviewing schema.org documentation will help ensure you're utilizing new features or best practices that emerge over time—keeping you ahead of competitors who may overlook this vital aspect of SEO strategy.

Incorporating structured data has transitioned from being an optional enhancement to a necessary strategy for enhancing digital presence in today's competitive landscape. As this component continues gaining traction within SEO circles, its thoughtful implementation will enrich user experiences and pave the way for sustained organic growth for businesses navigating the complexities of modern digital marketing.

Technical Tools for SEO Audits

Technical SEO audits are essential to a successful SEO strategy, providing a thorough evaluation of your website's infrastructure to ensure it follows best practices for maximizing visibility in search engines. To conduct these audits effectively, it's crucial to understand the various tools available that can offer insights into your site's performance and highlight areas for improvement.

Start with Google Search Console, a powerful resource offered by Google. This tool allows you to monitor your site's presence in search results and identifies issues like crawl errors, index coverage problems, and mobile usability concerns. By exploring the "Coverage" section, you can determine which pages are indexed and identify any obstacles preventing others from being crawled. Take this example, if you see an "Error" status on a key page, resolving that issue can significantly boost your organic traffic.

Another invaluable tool is Screaming Frog SEO Spider, a desktop application that crawls websites to provide detailed analyses of various elements such as meta tags, headings, and image alt attributes. Running a crawl with Screaming Frog gives you insights into missing or duplicate title tags, broken links, and on-page elements needing optimization. This data allows you to prioritize pages that require immediate attention.

Additionally, consider using PageSpeed Insights to assess your website's load speed and performance metrics. It offers actionable recommendations based on Google's Core Web Vitals, which will be crucial for ranking in 2025 and beyond. For example, if PageSpeed Insights indicates that your largest contentful paint (LCP) exceeds the recommended threshold, optimizing images or improving server response times can enhance both user experience and search rankings.

Ahrefs and SEMrush are standout platforms for comprehensive SEO analysis and competitor research. Ahrefs' Site Audit tool scans your site for over 100 potential performance and technical issues, while SEMrush not only provides site auditing features but also enables you to track keyword rankings and analyze competitors' strategies. Take this example, running an audit might reveal numerous broken internal links; fixing these can enhance user experience and improve crawling efficiency.

When conducting an audit, don't overlook mobile-friendliness. Google's Mobile-Friendly Test is an excellent resource to determine how easily users can access your content on mobile devices. With mobile-first indexing becoming the norm, ensuring your site is optimized for mobile users is essential.

GTmetrix is another valuable tool that combines Google PageSpeed Insights and YSlow metrics for a comprehensive view of page performance. Beyond basic numbers, GTmetrix offers tailored recommendations for improving loading times—such as implementing browser caching strategies or minifying CSS files.

Once you have collected data from these tools, the next step is to synthesize this information into actionable insights. Create an audit report that summarizes key findings: categorize issues by severity (critical versus minor), assign responsibilities for addressing them, and set timelines for implementation.

For practical execution of these findings, prioritize high-impact areas first—such as fixing broken links or optimizing page speed —before moving on to more granular issues like tweaking meta descriptions or adjusting header tags. As you address each point raised during the audit process, document the changes made and monitor any shifts in traffic or rankings through analytics tools like Google Analytics.

regular technical audits are vital for maintaining a healthy website in an ever-evolving digital landscape. As algorithms change and user expectations grow more sophisticated, having reliable tools at your disposal empowers you to stay ahead of potential pitfalls while continually improving your site's overall performance.

Technical audits not only reveal existing problems; they also uncover opportunities for growth and innovation in how users engage with your content online. By embracing this proactive approach, you can elevate your site's search engine performance and enhance the overall user experience—critical factors for success in the competitive SEO environment of 2025.

CHAPTER 6: THE IMPACT OF AI AND MACHINE LEARNING ON SEO

Introduction to AI in SEO

The integration of artificial intelligence (AI) into SEO represents a significant transformation in digital marketing strategies. The era of relying solely on manual data analysis and keyword stuffing is behind us. Today, AI enables marketers to tap into vast amounts of data, uncovering insights that were previously out of reach and facilitating hyper-personalized user experiences.

At the heart of AI's role in SEO is its enhanced ability to analyze user behavior patterns far more effectively than traditional methods. Take this example, machine learning algorithms can monitor engagement metrics across diverse demographics, allowing marketers to craft content strategies that resonate profoundly with their target audiences. A prime example is Google's RankBrain, which utilizes AI to interpret search queries and refine results based on user interactions. When certain types of content consistently attract higher engagement, this information guides future content creation, ensuring alignment with audience preferences.

To illustrate the power of AI-driven insights, consider an e-commerce retailer that harnessed AI-powered analytics tools. By analyzing search trends, the company discovered a notable increase in demand for eco-friendly products. In response, they adjusted their inventory and optimized their website content accordingly. This strategic move resulted in a remarkable 40% increase in organic traffic over three months as users sought products that reflected their values.

Content generation also benefits greatly from AI advancements. Tools like OpenAI's GPT-3 have transformed how marketers produce written material. While human oversight remains crucial for maintaining brand voice, AI can assist in drafting blog posts or creating product descriptions from existing data inputs. This not only saves time but also streamlines the content production process. Imagine generating a series of blog outlines based on trending keywords within minutes instead of hours.

However, leveraging AI comes with its own set of challenges, particularly concerning ethics. As machine learning increasingly informs decision-making processes in SEO strategies, it's vital to remain transparent about user data usage and ensure compliance with regulations like GDPR. Striking a balance between innovation and ethical responsibility fosters trust among your audience as you integrate AI into your SEO practices.

Predictive analytics is another game-changer that enables marketers to anticipate future trends based on historical data analysis. By employing AI-driven predictive models, businesses can forecast shifts in consumer behavior or search trends before they arise. Take this example, if past data indicates a spike in interest for remote work-related products every January due to New Year resolutions, companies can optimize their marketing strategies accordingly—potentially launching targeted campaigns ahead of the curve.

Where X meets Y natural language processing (NLP) and SEO further underscores the transformative impact of AI technologies. Search engines are becoming increasingly adept at understanding the context and intent behind queries rather than merely matching keywords. This evolution makes producing high-quality, contextually relevant content more essential than ever. Marketers should prioritize creating comprehensive resources that address specific user needs instead of relying solely on keyword-centric writing.

In practical terms, optimizing for voice search—a domain where NLP excels—is becoming increasingly important as more users engage with devices like Amazon Alexa or Google Assistant daily. Crafting conversational content that succinctly answers common questions enhances the likelihood of being featured in voice search results.

As we explore the growing influence of AI in SEO practices, it's clear that staying updated with technological advancements is essential for anyone serious about succeeding in digital marketing today. This commitment involves continually learning about emerging tools and methodologies while remaining flexible in strategy execution.

To wrap things up, understanding and integrating artificial intelligence into your SEO practices is not just beneficial; it's essential for thriving in an increasingly competitive landscape. Embracing these innovations allows you to transform raw data into actionable insights while enhancing user experiences through personalized interactions and targeted content delivery. Mastering these technologies will ultimately shape your effectiveness as an SEO strategist as we navigate this new digital frontier together.

Machine Learning and Personalization

Machine learning has fundamentally transformed the landscape of SEO, shifting strategies from reactive to proactive. By leveraging algorithms that learn and adapt, marketers can refine their approaches to better cater to their audiences. This evolution goes beyond mere automation; it signifies a paradigm shift in how we understand and anticipate user behavior.

Search engines now analyze vast datasets to identify what content resonates with users. Machine learning models sift through metrics like clicks, dwell time, and engagement levels, enabling marketers to craft strategies grounded in solid evidence rather than guesswork. Take this example, when a blog post about sustainable living gains traction among eco-conscious consumers, machine learning can quickly detect this trend. So, marketers can pivot their content strategy to produce more articles on related topics, capitalizing on this newfound interest.

Personalization exemplifies the strength of machine learning. The ability to deliver tailored content recommendations significantly enhances user experience. Platforms such as Netflix and Spotify employ sophisticated algorithms to suggest shows or songs based on individual preferences and habits. In the SEO context, businesses can adopt similar techniques to provide personalized product recommendations or content suggestions on their websites. An online bookstore might analyze past purchase data and browsing behavior to highlight new releases that align with each user's interests—this level of customization can lead to markedly higher conversion rates.

To implement machine learning effectively, marketers must first grasp the data available to them. Tools like Google Analytics and AI-driven analytics platforms offer insights into user behaviors and preferences. Marketers should prioritize key performance indicators (KPIs) such as click-through rates (CTR), bounce rates, and conversion rates. By analyzing these metrics, businesses can uncover patterns in user interactions that guide future content creation and optimization efforts.

For example, a travel website could utilize machine learning algorithms to examine seasonal trends in search queries. If data shows an uptick in interest for winter holiday destinations during October, the site can proactively optimize content around those keywords and develop targeted marketing campaigns before competitors seize the opportunity.

The rise of voice search further highlights the importance of personalization through machine learning. As more users rely on devices like smartphones and smart speakers for information, search engines prioritize results that align with conversational queries. Crafting content that directly addresses user intent—by using natural language—is crucial. Instead of merely focusing on "best hiking trails," incorporating phrases such as "What are the best hiking trails for families?" effectively responds to specific questions.

Machine learning also enables A/B testing at an unprecedented scale. Marketers can automate tests of different headlines or images on landing pages to determine which variants yield higher engagement results. This iterative process allows teams to make swift, data-driven decisions while continuously optimizing performance based on real-time feedback.

However, integrating machine learning into SEO strategies does present challenges. It requires a robust foundation of quality data and an understanding of algorithm functionality. Ethical considerations regarding data privacy are paramount; businesses must prioritize transparency in how they collect and use customer information while complying with regulations like GDPR.

mastering machine learning's capabilities in SEO provides a competitive edge in today's digital landscape. As we move toward a future where personalization becomes essential, embracing these technologies will be vital for anyone seeking to develop effective marketing strategies that deeply resonate with their audience.

By transforming data into actionable insights through machine learning, marketers are not just responding to trends but actively shaping them—positioning themselves as leaders in their respective fields. This ongoing evolution underscores the importance of remaining agile and informed as we collectively navigate the complexities of SEO's future.

Analyzing Search Engine AI Algorithms

Search engines have transformed into complex systems powered by artificial intelligence algorithms. These algorithms not only index and retrieve information but also learn from user interactions to improve search results. For an SEO strategy to succeed in the competitive landscape of 2025, it is essential to grasp how these algorithms function. Essentially of this understanding is a commitment to unraveling the mechanics of search engine AI, which can revolutionize marketing strategies and significantly enhance visibility and engagement.

The first step in analyzing search engine algorithms is recognizing their dependence on vast amounts of data. Every day, algorithms sift through billions of queries, identifying patterns that help refine results. For example, Google's RankBrain employs machine learning to process search queries, enabling it to grasp not just keywords but also their context. When a user inputs a vague query like "best Italian food," RankBrain interprets the intent behind the search, considering factors such as geographic location and past searches to deliver relevant restaurant recommendations. This advanced processing underscores why keyword stuffing has become obsolete; understanding user intent is now paramount.

To put this knowledge into practice, marketers must focus on creating comprehensive, well-structured content that addresses specific questions users are likely to ask. Take this example, a restaurant owner could write an article titled "Top 10 Family-Friendly Italian Restaurants in [City]" rather than simply targeting the term "Italian food." This approach anticipates user needs and aligns with how algorithms rank content based on relevance and usefulness.

A deeper exploration of how algorithms interpret content leads us to Natural Language Processing (NLP), a branch of AI that allows machines to comprehend human language. The launch of Google's BERT (Bidirectional Encoder Representations from Transformers) marked a pivotal change in how search engines understand language nuances. With BERT, even complex questions can be interpreted more effectively, as it breaks them down into contextually relevant components.

To stay ahead in this evolving landscape, marketers must adapt their strategies accordingly. This adaptation includes structuring content with clear headers and bullet points to enhance readability—elements that not only improve user experience but also align with algorithms' preference for scannable content. By presenting information in digestible formats while maintaining rich detail and relevance, businesses can boost their chances of achieving higher rankings in search engine results pages (SERPs).

Another crucial factor to consider is the role of user engagement signals. Algorithms evaluate user interactions—such as click-through rates (CTR) and time spent on page—to assess content quality. If a blog post receives high CTR but low dwell time, it may suggest a disconnect between user expectations and the content provided. For example, if users anticipate an article about family-friendly dining options but encounter technical jargon or overly complex explanations about cuisine styles instead, they are likely to return swiftly to the results page.

To address this issue, businesses can utilize tools like heatmaps or session recordings from platforms such as Hotjar or Crazy Egg. These tools provide insights into user behavior—showing where visitors click most often and where they lose interest —enabling marketers to adapt their content strategy based on real-time data.

Additionally, as mobile usage continues to rise, search engines are prioritizing local intent more than ever. Algorithms are increasingly fine-tuned to deliver localized results effectively. A small café might optimize its Google My Business listing by including current photos, operational hours, menu items, and engaging descriptions that reflect local culture or nearby events. This way, they not only provide valuable information but also signal relevance and timeliness—key considerations for AI-driven search engines focused on delivering meaningful results.

Navigating the complexities of AI-driven changes also involves ensuring compliance with privacy regulations like GDPR. With search engines under scrutiny regarding data usage, transparency becomes crucial for building trust with users while still benefiting from personalized marketing strategies.

To wrap things up, examining search engine AI algorithms reveals a rapidly evolving digital landscape driven by context understanding rather than mere keyword matching. With each update providing deeper insights into user behavior patterns and preferences, leveraging this knowledge enables marketers not only to meet expectations but also to exceed them creatively. This approach fosters experiences that resonate with target audiences while enhancing overall brand visibility in search results.

As these algorithms continue to refine themselves through advanced learning techniques, understanding their inner workings will be vital for anyone seeking sustained success in SEO practices moving into 2025 and beyond.

Natural Language Processing in SEO

Natural Language Processing (NLP) has revolutionized how search engines understand and respond to user queries. To fully appreciate its impact on SEO, we must recognize that NLP enables machines to interpret human language with greater nuance. This transformation goes beyond simple keyword matching; it involves understanding context, intent, and sentiment. Take this example, when a user searches for "best coffee shops near me," the search engine analyzes the underlying intent rather than just the specific words, looking for recommendations based on location and quality.

The role of NLP in SEO is particularly significant as it reshapes our approach to search queries. The rise of voice search exemplifies this shift; users now tend to speak naturally rather than relying on fragmented keywords. When someone asks, "What's the best Italian restaurant around here?" the device must comprehend not only the key terms but also the implications of "best" and "around here." This evolution calls for a reevaluation of content structure, making it essential to optimize for conversational queries.

One effective way to harness the power of NLP is by incorporating natural language into your content. Rather than concentrating solely on specific keywords, focus on semantic relevance by using related terms and phrases that enrich your content's context. For example, if you're writing about coffee shops, include words like "café," "espresso," and "barista," as well as customer experiences and reviews. Technologies such as Google's BERT (Bidirectional Encoder Representations from Transformers) highlight how search engines now prioritize contextual understanding over exact matches.

In addition to this, optimizing for featured snippets offers another valuable opportunity where NLP plays a critical role. Featured snippets deliver direct answers to user queries at the top of search results and are often sourced from well-structured content that addresses questions clearly. To take advantage of this feature, structure your content with clear headings, bullet points, and concise answers to common questions within your niche. For example, if your blog focuses on healthy eating, directly answer questions like "What are the benefits of quinoa?" in visually distinct paragraphs.

Employing structured data markup can also enhance your

content's visibility. Schema markup allows you to specify elements such as reviews, recipes, events, or products. By adding this layer of information, you help search engines better understand your content's context, ultimately leading to more relevant results for users and improved visibility in search outcomes.

Another interesting area to explore is sentiment analysis— a facet of NLP that evaluates emotional tone within user-generated content such as reviews or social media posts. Gaining insight into sentiment can inform your content strategy effectively. If you notice negative feedback about certain aspects of your product or service in reviews, addressing these concerns transparently can bolster your brand image and foster customer loyalty.

As NLP continues to advance, staying updated on its developments is crucial for maintaining an effective SEO strategy. Regularly engaging with industry updates or following thought leaders who explore AI and machine learning applications in digital marketing will keep you informed. By integrating these insights into your strategy, you position yourself ahead of competitors who may still rely on outdated practices.

Embracing Natural Language Processing is no longer optional; it's essential for success in today's competitive landscape. As algorithms become increasingly adept at understanding human interactions with technology, our strategies must also evolve. The goal is not just adaptation but thriving through creativity and innovation in our SEO practices—ultimately fostering deeper connections between users and brands online.

Predictive Analytics for SEO Strategy

Predictive analytics has become a transformative force in SEO strategies, enabling marketers to anticipate user behavior and refine their approaches accordingly. By harnessing historical data and statistical algorithms, businesses can forecast trends, gauge user engagement, and identify potential search patterns. This shift from reactive to proactive strategies fundamentally changes how we approach SEO.

At the heart of predictive analytics is the understanding of data collected from various sources. User interactions—such as clicks, time spent on pages, and conversion rates—offer invaluable insights. For example, if a website observes a surge in traffic for specific product categories during particular seasons or events, it can proactively prepare content and marketing campaigns to capitalize on these trends. Take an e-commerce site specializing in outdoor gear; as summer approaches, a spike in searches for hiking equipment may prompt it to optimize product pages and launch targeted promotions ahead of peak shopping times.

To facilitate this analysis, tools like Google Analytics and advanced platforms such as IBM Watson or Salesforce Einstein are invaluable. These tools enable businesses to segment their audience based on behaviors and preferences. Take this example, using Google Analytics' audience segmentation feature allows you to analyze how different demographics engage with your content. If younger users are showing a preference for video content over written articles, you might adjust your strategy to include more video marketing targeted at that demographic.

Implementing predictive models is another vital component of this approach. Machine learning algorithms can sift through large datasets to uncover patterns that might elude human analysts. For example, if you manage a travel blog, employing predictive analytics can help you model trends around travel destinations based on user searches from the previous year or current social media buzz. This foresight enables you to create content that aligns with emerging interests before they gain mainstream traction.

Keyword forecasting is also essential within your predictive analytics framework. Rather than solely focusing on existing high-volume keywords, it's crucial to analyze how keyword popularity evolves over time. Tools like SEMrush or Ahrefs offer keyword tracking features that help identify rising search terms within your niche. Take this example, if "sustainable travel" starts to trend upward in search queries, it signals an opportunity for you to develop relevant content that addresses this growing interest.

Predictive analytics enhances SEO by optimizing content based on expected performance metrics as well. Conducting A/B tests on different headlines or descriptions can reveal which variations resonate most effectively with users. This ongoing testing allows for continuous optimization of web pages based on real-time data rather than mere assumptions.

The relationship between user intent and predictive analytics is another critical area to consider. Understanding the context behind search queries helps create tailored content that meets user needs effectively. For example, if data shows an increasing number of searches for "best budget laptops" compared to "high-end laptops," your content strategy should shift focus toward comparative reviews and budget-friendly recommendations instead of premium offerings.

Incorporating social media trends into your predictive analytics framework can further enhance your insights. Social listening tools track mentions of relevant topics across platforms like Twitter and Instagram. If you notice a surge in conversations about wellness retreats online, timely blog posts or landing pages centered around this theme could capture organic traffic while interest is high.

As we delve deeper into leveraging predictive analytics for SEO strategy development, regular evaluations become essential for maintaining alignment with user behaviors and market shifts. Establishing key performance indicators (KPIs) will help measure the effectiveness of your predictions against actual outcomes, guiding necessary adjustments for future campaigns.

Staying ahead in SEO requires not just responding but anticipating changes—this is where predictive analytics truly excels. It transforms raw data into strategic insights that inform decisions based on foresight rather than hindsight alone. Embracing these analytical capabilities is crucial for forging pathways toward success in modern SEO practices amid an ever-evolving landscape where anticipation creates opportunity.

Content Optimization with AI

Content optimization through AI is not just an enhancement of existing strategies; it signifies a fundamental shift in how we create and deliver content. As the digital landscape continues to evolve, harnessing artificial intelligence allows marketers to personalize content in unprecedented ways, crafting experiences that resonate deeply with users. This transformation begins with an understanding of AI's capabilities in analyzing user data, predicting behavior, and generating relevant content.

AI tools excel at sifting through vast amounts of data to uncover patterns in user engagement. For example, platforms like Clearscope and MarketMuse employ natural language processing (NLP) to analyze top-performing content within specific niches. By examining keywords, topics, and user sentiment, these tools provide guidance on creating articles that align with SEO best practices while meeting the nuanced needs of your audience. Imagine managing a health blog: rather than randomly selecting topics, you could leverage AI insights to focus on trending health issues or dietary preferences among your readers, ensuring your content stays relevant and engaging.

Another significant advantage of AI in content optimization is its ability to automate repetitive tasks. Tools such as Grammarly and Copy.ai offer suggestions for enhancing writing style, grammar, and overall structure. This efficiency allows writers to concentrate more on creativity and strategy instead of getting caught up in technical details. Take this example, when drafting product descriptions for an e-commerce site, AI can provide optimized templates that highlight key features and benefits while ensuring that each description appeals to both search engines and potential buyers.

Personalization works hand-in-hand with content optimization when utilizing AI technologies. By analyzing user behavior on your website—such as which articles they read or products they view—AI systems can help create dynamic content experiences. For example, if a visitor frequently explores articles about plant-based diets on a food blog, AI can recommend related recipes or products tailored specifically to those interests. This targeted approach not only enhances user experience but also increases the likelihood of conversions by presenting relevant information at the right moment.

AI-driven analytics further empower marketers to refine their content strategies continuously. Tools like HubSpot and Google Data Studio allow you to monitor the performance of different pieces of content across various channels. If a blog post titled "5 Easy Vegan Recipes" attracts significantly more traffic than others, it may signal an opportunity to produce similar themed posts or even expand into video tutorials that showcase these recipes in action.

The optimization process extends beyond content creation; it also encompasses distribution. AI algorithms can predict the optimal times and platforms for sharing your content based on historical audience engagement data. For example, if analysis shows that most of your audience interacts with social media posts during late afternoons, scheduling posts for this timeframe can boost visibility and interaction rates.

As AI continues to advance, its role in optimizing multimedia elements—such as images and videos—within your content strategy becomes increasingly important. Tools like Canva are integrating AI features that suggest design enhancements or layout changes based on current trends and user preferences. Ensuring that visual assets align seamlessly with written content maximizes engagement across diverse platforms.

Incorporating feedback loops into your optimization strategy is crucial for ongoing improvement. By employing machine learning algorithms to analyze user interactions—like click-through rates or time spent on a page—you can adjust your approach dynamically. Take this example, if analytics reveal that users abandon an article halfway through due to a lack of engaging visuals, you can strategize to include infographics or video snippets that maintain interest throughout the piece.

adopting an AI-centric approach to content optimization transforms SEO from a static practice into a dynamic dialogue with users. By understanding their needs and leveraging data-driven insights, marketers can craft compelling narratives that resonate long after users leave their websites. As you integrate these advanced techniques into your SEO strategies, remember that the goal is not only visibility but also building meaningful connections that drive loyalty and conversions over time. This evolution towards intelligent content generation positions brands as leaders in their fields while addressing real-world challenges faced by their audiences today.

Using AI Tools and Platforms

Artificial intelligence (AI) tools are rapidly becoming essential for modern marketers, offering capabilities that streamline workflows and enhance content effectiveness. Incorporating AI into SEO strategies is not just about staying current; it's about harnessing advanced technology to transform content creation and distribution. This journey begins with identifying the right tools that align with your specific needs and objectives.

Start by familiarizing yourself with platforms like SEMrush, Ahrefs, and Moz. These tools provide robust keyword research functionalities, enabling you to uncover high-value keywords that competitors may overlook. For example, if you run a travel blog focused on eco-tourism, these platforms can reveal long-tail keywords like "sustainable travel destinations 2025," appealing to an increasingly conscientious audience. By integrating these keywords naturally into your content, you enhance visibility while delivering value to your readers.

AI platforms also excel in competitive analysis. Tools like BuzzSumo allow you to identify which types of content perform best in your niche by analyzing social shares and engagement metrics. If you find that articles featuring "eco-friendly travel tips" garner significantly more shares, this insight can guide your content strategy toward producing similar high-engagement pieces. The goal is not just to create original content but to craft narratives that resonate with existing audience interests.

Another vital application of AI tools lies in automating outreach efforts. Solutions such as Mailchimp or HubSpot's marketing automation streamline email campaigns based on user behavior patterns. Imagine targeting users who clicked on your recent newsletter article about eco-tourism with a personalized follow-up email featuring exclusive discounts for eco-friendly vacation packages. This targeted communication boosts engagement rates and fosters a deeper connection with your audience.

AI-driven chatbots are revolutionizing interactions with website visitors as well. Platforms like Drift or Intercom provide real-time assistance, guiding users to relevant information or addressing inquiries instantly. Take this example, if a visitor arrives on your site seeking advice on sustainable hotels, a well-programmed chatbot can offer tailored suggestions based on previous interactions or frequently asked questions, enhancing the user experience and increasing conversion likelihood.

Leveraging user-generated content (UGC) is another area where AI shines. Platforms like Yotpo facilitate the efficient collection of reviews and testimonials, showcasing authentic customer experiences that enhance credibility and trustworthiness. Take this example, if you manage an e-commerce site selling sustainable travel gear, integrating UGC can significantly enrich product pages and serve as powerful social proof that influences purchasing decisions.

And, ensuring your content is optimized across various formats is crucial in today's multi-channel environment. Tools like Hootsuite help manage social media posting effectively while utilizing AI insights to determine optimal engagement times across different platforms—whether it's Instagram for visuals or LinkedIn for professional insights into sustainable practices in travel.

As we move into an increasingly AI-centric era of SEO, remember that these tools are not just enhancements; they are essential allies in understanding and connecting with your audience on a deeper level. Each tool has its unique strengths; the key is selecting those that align with your goals while maintaining a consistent brand voice across all channels.

Integrating AI into your marketing toolkit goes beyond mere efficiency; it empowers you to craft richer narratives and forge deeper connections with users who are becoming more discerning about their online choices. With every click analyzed and every interaction optimized through intelligent automation, you're not only equipped to meet current demands but also to anticipate future ones—transforming data-driven insights into actionable strategies that keep you ahead in the competitive landscape of SEO.

The Ethics of AI in Search

Artificial intelligence (AI) is more than just a tool in your SEO toolkit; it has the potential to transform your entire digital marketing strategy. However, as we embrace the power of AI, we must also confront the ethical considerations that accompany its integration. Striking a balance between leveraging AI's remarkable capabilities and adhering to ethical standards requires careful reflection and intentional decision-making.

One key area to consider is data usage. With access to extensive user data, AI algorithms can analyze behavior patterns, preferences, and demographics to optimize SEO efforts. Yet, there is a delicate balance between using this data for personalization and respecting privacy rights. For example, while customizing content recommendations based on a user's browsing history can enhance engagement, transparency about data collection and usage is crucial. Educating users about their rights and providing clear privacy policies can help alleviate concerns regarding data misuse.

Ethical considerations also extend to content creation. AI-generated content tools can produce articles, product descriptions, and social media posts at remarkable speeds. However, over-reliance on these tools without proper oversight risks generating low-quality or misleading information. As an SEO professional, it's essential to prioritize authenticity and accuracy over mere volume. Take this example, when using AI to create blog posts on travel safety during crises, it's vital to verify facts and offer valuable insights rather than depending solely on algorithms for content generation.

Bias in AI systems presents another pressing ethical challenge. Since algorithms learn from existing data, any biases inherent in that data can be perpetuated in search results or recommendations. For example, an e-commerce site focused on eco-friendly products might rank lower due to biased keyword analysis based on historical trends. To mitigate this risk, regularly auditing your AI tools for bias in their outputs is crucial. Engaging diverse teams in developing content strategies helps ensure various perspectives are represented and reduces the likelihood of excluding important voices.

The ethical use of AI also impacts brand-consumer interactions. While chatbots can quickly respond to customer inquiries, if they fail to provide empathetic and contextually relevant answers, they may frustrate users instead of enhancing their experience. Creating conversational models that emulate human understanding requires ongoing refinement informed by user feedback.

Additionally, automation in outreach efforts comes with its own set of challenges. Although automation allows for efficient communication with large audiences through personalized emails or messages based on previous interactions, neglecting the human touch can lead to negative experiences. A well-timed follow-up email should feel personal rather than robotic; thus, finding the right balance between automation and genuine human engagement is essential.

Building trust through transparency in your use of AI solutions is critical as consumers become increasingly skeptical about digital marketing tactics. Clearly communicating when users are interacting with AI-driven processes—such as chatbots or algorithm-based recommendations—reinforces trustworthiness and enhances the overall experience.

Navigating the ethical landscape of AI requires diligence but also offers an opportunity to establish industry standards grounded in integrity. Leading by example not only elevates your brand's reputation but also contributes positively to the broader conversation surrounding ethics in technology.

To wrap things up, adopting a responsible approach to AI integration positions you as a forward-thinking leader in SEO practices while honoring the values cherished by your audience. By blending advanced technology with ethical considerations, you lay the groundwork for sustainable success—an essential element for thriving in today's fast-evolving digital marketplace where integrity is as valuable as innovation.

CHAPTER 7: CONTENT IS KING: CREATING HIGH- QUALITY CONTENT

Content Creation Strategies

C ontent creation in SEO has evolved beyond the simple strategy of stuffing pages with keywords. Today, it requires a thoughtful blend of creativity and data-driven insights to produce content that resonates with both users and search engines. To excel in this arena, you need a comprehensive strategy that addresses multiple aspects of content creation.

Start by pinpointing your audience's needs, as understanding who you are writing for is fundamental to effective content creation. Developing buyer personas—detailed profiles of your ideal customers based on market research and real data— can provide valuable insights. For example, if your target demographic includes tech-savvy millennials interested in sustainable products, your content should reflect their values and language. Consider creating blog posts about eco-friendly gadgets, incorporating relatable examples and engaging visuals to draw them in.

Next, think about the types of content that will best engage your audience. This could include in-depth articles, how-to guides, videos, or infographics. By diversifying your content formats, you cater to various learning styles and enhance overall engagement. If you run a health blog, for instance, complementing written articles with video tutorials on exercise routines or healthy cooking can add significant value for visual learners.

Maintaining a consistent voice and tone across all your content is equally important for building brand recognition and trust. Establish a style guide that outlines your preferred vocabulary, tone, and messaging framework. A fitness brand targeting young adults might adopt an energetic, motivational voice, while a financial advisory service may opt for a more formal and authoritative approach. Tailoring your voice to meet audience expectations strengthens the connection you have with them.

As you create content, focus on quality over quantity. Google increasingly prioritizes well-researched, authoritative articles over generic filler. Conduct thorough research before writing; utilize tools like SEMrush or Ahrefs to gather relevant statistics and insights. For example, if you're addressing the impact of sleep on mental health, including recent studies or expert quotes can lend credibility to your work.

Seamlessly integrating search engine optimization into your content strategy is essential as well. This involves effective keyword usage without sacrificing readability. Begin by identifying primary keywords through comprehensive research tools like Google Keyword Planner or Ubersuggest. If "sleep hygiene" is a high-traffic keyword in the mental health niche, ensure it appears naturally within headings and throughout the text while maintaining smooth flow.

Another critical aspect of SEO-driven content creation is incorporating internal and external links. Internal links help guide readers to related content on your website, enhancing user experience and encouraging longer engagement—an important factor for improving SEO rankings. Take this example, if you have an article about sleep hygiene tips, linking it to another piece discussing common sleep disorders provides readers with additional valuable information.

Don't underestimate the importance of compelling headlines and introductions; first impressions are crucial. Your headlines should grab attention while accurately reflecting the essence of the content. Tools like CoSchedule's Headline Analyzer can assist you in crafting headlines that entice clicks without resorting to clickbait tactics.

Once you've published your content, promoting it is vital to maximize its reach. Share it across social media platforms where your audience congregates; consider using email newsletters or collaborating with influencers in your niche to boost visibility further. Hosting a joint webinar featuring industry experts can attract attention while establishing authority within the community.

Analyzing performance metrics after publication is crucial for continuous improvement. Tools like Google Analytics provide insights into user behavior—such as how long visitors stay on the page and which sections engage them most—informing future strategies. If you observe users bouncing from a particular article on sleep hygiene tips, revisit that content for optimization based on feedback.

As you refine these strategies over time, remember that creativity plays an essential role in distinguishing yourself amidst digital noise. Experimenting with storytelling techniques or interactive elements can set your brand apart from competitors targeting similar audiences.

Encouraging user-generated content can also enhance authenticity and engagement levels; invite customers to share their experiences with your products or services through reviews or social media posts featuring branded hashtags.

an effective content creation strategy harmonizes data-driven insights with creativity and a genuine understanding of audience needs—positioning you as both an authority in SEO and a trusted source of information within your niche. Each piece of content serves as a building block toward establishing deeper connections with users while driving traffic to your site —making every effort worthwhile in today's digital landscape where valuable relationships lead to success.

The Role of Editorial Calendars

Content creation is a multifaceted endeavor that requires careful planning and execution. At the heart of this process lies the editorial calendar, which serves as a guiding framework to ensure that your content aligns with strategic objectives and meets audience expectations. By organizing your content schedule, you create a clear roadmap that enhances both creativity and efficiency.

An editorial calendar allows you to visualize your content strategy over time. Begin by identifying key themes or topics relevant to your audience. For example, if you manage a travel blog, you might outline content related to seasonal travel trends —highlighting summer vacations in early spring or winter getaways as the holidays approach. This proactive approach enables you to capitalize on timely searches while keeping your content fresh and engaging.

Incorporating significant events or dates into your calendar can further enhance relevance. Aligning your content with industry events, holidays, or awareness months creates opportunities for high-traffic keywords and demonstrates your engagement with current conversations in your field. Take this example, if you're running a health and wellness website, planning articles around National Nutrition Month in March or Mental Health Awareness Month in May can resonate strongly with your audience.

A well-structured editorial calendar also facilitates team

collaboration. If you work with multiple contributors—such as writers, designers, or social media managers—an organized framework clarifies roles and deadlines. Tools like Trello or Asana can help you assign tasks and track progress visually. For example, if a new article on sustainable travel is scheduled for publication in two weeks, you can designate specific responsibilities like research, writing, and graphic design to different team members while keeping everyone informed about deadlines.

Regularly reviewing and updating your editorial calendar is crucial for maintaining flexibility. The digital landscape evolves quickly; staying ahead requires agility. If a viral topic emerges unexpectedly—such as a newly popular travel destination—being able to insert timely content can position you as a thought leader. Consider creating buffer space within your calendar for spontaneous content opportunities without compromising previously planned pieces.

Another significant advantage of using an editorial calendar is the ability to optimize for search engine visibility. By planning content around target keywords identified during research sessions, you ensure that each piece serves a dual purpose: engaging users while meeting SEO criteria. Take this example, if "eco-friendly travel tips" is trending among searches related to sustainable tourism, structure your articles accordingly and weave relevant keywords naturally throughout.

In addition to keyword optimization, leverage analytics from past posts when filling out your calendar. Analyzing which topics have driven traffic or engagement can inform future content decisions significantly. If an article on solo travel received considerable attention last year, expanding that topic into a series could be beneficial.

Compelling headlines also warrant special attention within your editorial structure. As you draft titles for upcoming pieces, test them against headline analyzers like CoSchedule's tool or Sharethrough's Headline Analyzer to assess their potential effectiveness before publication. Strong headlines not only entice clicks but also set the stage for user engagement from the moment visitors arrive on your page.

And, a well-planned editorial calendar makes it easier to interlink published articles. As you produce new content on similar themes or related topics over time, linking them creates a cohesive body of work that enhances user experience and improves SEO performance through increased dwell time on site pages.

Lastly, don't overlook the importance of promotion strategies within your calendar framework. Designate specific times for social media sharing and cross-promotion based on when your audience is most active. For example, if Instagram sees higher engagement rates in the evenings during weekdays for your target demographic, plan to release visual teasers linked back to blog posts at those peak times.

In summary, effectively utilizing an editorial calendar streamlines the content creation process while enhancing strategic alignment across all facets of digital marketing efforts. It fosters collaboration among teams and provides the agility needed to respond swiftly to changing trends—all while ensuring consistent quality and relevance that resonates with audiences amid growing online competition. When managed diligently, an editorial calendar becomes more than just a schedule; it evolves into a dynamic tool that drives engagement and establishes authority within any niche.

Writing for Your Audience

Writing for your audience is the foundation of effective content creation. To truly connect with your readers, it's essential to understand who they are, what they seek, and how they communicate. This understanding informs not just your choice of topics but also the voice and tone you use. By focusing on these elements, you can foster a more meaningful connection with your audience, leading to engagement and loyalty that builds lasting relationships.

Begin by creating audience personas—fictional representations of your ideal readers grounded in real data and insights. Take this example, if you're targeting a tech-savvy demographic interested in cybersecurity, you might develop a persona like "Tech-Savvy Tara." In her late 30s and working in IT, Tara primarily consumes content through podcasts and articles. This persona serves as a guiding framework for decisions regarding content types, styles, and distribution channels.

With your personas established, delve into their specific needs and pain points. Consider the challenges they face that your content can address. For example, "Tech-Savvy Tara" may feel anxious about emerging cybersecurity threats. Your articles should not only inform but also provide actionable solutions tailored to her situation—such as step-by-step guides for enhancing personal cybersecurity or insights into the latest threat detection technologies.

Next, think about the tone and style that will resonate with your audience. A lighthearted approach may suit a lifestyle blog, while a more formal tone might be appropriate for a financial services site. Your language should align with both your audience's expectations and the subject matter at hand. Tools like Grammarly or Hemingway can assist in refining your writing for clarity and impact.

In addition to tone, consider formatting and accessibility. Breaking up text with headings, bullet points, and images caters to readers who prefer skimming rather than deep reading. Research shows that many online readers favor easily digestible content; structuring your articles with these elements enhances reader retention. Take this example, outlining key steps in a process using bullet points allows quick access to information without requiring readers to wade through dense paragraphs.

Engaging storytelling is another powerful tool when writing

for your audience. Personal anecdotes or case studies can make complex topics relatable. If you're discussing marketing strategies for small businesses, sharing a success story from a local café that effectively leveraged social media illustrates practical applications of theoretical concepts.

When developing content, prioritize quality over quantity. One insightful piece that addresses pressing questions will outperform several mediocre articles filled with fluff. This principle is increasingly relevant as search engines prioritize quality content; ensuring each article provides real value can significantly boost SEO performance.

Incorporate user feedback into your writing process as well. Engaging with your audience through comments or social media can offer valuable insights into their preferences and interests. If readers frequently ask questions about specific aspects of your topic, addressing those queries directly in future articles helps establish you as an authority while catering to their curiosity.

Finally, utilize analytics tools to gauge how well your content resonates with readers after publication. Google Analytics provides insights into user behavior—monitoring metrics like bounce rates or time spent on page enables you to identify which pieces engage audiences most effectively. For example, if an article on "Best Cybersecurity Practices" attracts significantly higher traffic than others, consider creating follow-up pieces or related resources to capitalize on that interest.

writing for your audience is an ongoing process of learning and adapting. It transcends merely delivering information; it involves crafting experiences that resonate deeply with readers' needs and aspirations. By grounding your approach in research, engaging narratives, clear formatting, and continuous feedback loops, you can create compelling content that captures attention and drives meaningful interactions in any digital space. This dedication to understanding your audience will set you apart as a trusted source amid the noise of online information overload.

Content Formats and Their Impact

Content formats are essential in determining how your audience perceives, understands, and engages with information. Each format comes with its own set of advantages and limitations, making the selection process crucial for achieving your objectives and resonating with your target readers. Take this example, infographics can simplify complex data into visually appealing designs, while videos captivate viewers through dynamic storytelling. Familiarity with these various formats enables you to craft a more effective content strategy.

In today's digital landscape, visual content holds significant sway. Research indicates that articles featuring images receive 94% more views than those without. This shows the importance of integrating visuals that not only complement but also enhance your written content. When presenting statistics or data, using charts or graphs can provide clarity at a glance. Tools like Canva allow you to create stunning visuals easily, even if you lack advanced design skills. Engaging visuals not only make your content more interesting but also improve retention; readers are more likely to remember visual elements than plain text.

Audio formats, such as podcasts and voiceovers, also play a vital role, particularly for audiences who prefer auditory learning experiences. With over 50% of Americans having listened to a podcast, this format offers an excellent opportunity to broaden your reach. For example, if you're discussing SEO strategies for e-commerce businesses, hosting a podcast series featuring industry experts can offer valuable insights while fostering community engagement.

For written content, blog posts remain a cornerstone of content marketing. However, the style and structure can vary significantly depending on the intent behind each piece. Long-form content is ideal for in-depth explorations of topics—perfect for comprehensive guides or detailed analyses—while short-form pieces serve well for quick updates or news articles that demand immediacy and brevity. Integrating both styles into your strategy can be beneficial; for instance, you might create an extensive guide on local SEO tactics alongside shorter updates that address current industry developments.

Webinars present another effective format that combines visual presentations with interactive components. They provide a platform not only to showcase your expertise but also to engage participants in real-time through Q&A sessions. If you're launching a new product or service, hosting a webinar can generate immediate feedback while informing potential customers about its features and benefits.

To maximize the effectiveness of each format, strategic promotion across appropriate channels is crucial. Social media platforms like Instagram and TikTok thrive on visual content, so repurposing blog posts into engaging videos or infographics tailored for these platforms can significantly expand your reach. In contrast, LinkedIn may be more suitable for professional articles or white papers that establish authority in your niche market.

As you diversify your content formats, it's important to monitor analytics to evaluate performance across different mediums. Tracking engagement metrics—such as likes, shares, and comments—can help you identify which formats resonate best with your audience. For example, if video tutorials garner significantly more engagement than text-based guides, consider increasing your video output while refining your written content strategy accordingly.

Beyond varying formats according to audience preferences and platform strengths, maintaining consistent branding across all content types is essential. Cohesive branding—through logo placement, color schemes, and tone of voice—fosters recognition and trust among your audience.

leveraging a mix of diverse content formats enhances user experience and positions you as an adaptable creator ready to meet diverse consumer needs in an ever-evolving digital landscape. The key lies in responsiveness: by continuously evaluating which formats yield the best results and adjusting your strategy accordingly, you can ensure that your content remains relevant and impactful over time.

Storytelling in SEO

In the world of SEO, storytelling has emerged as a powerful tool that transcends mere words. It involves crafting narratives that resonate with audiences, capturing their attention and driving engagement. This art form isn't exclusive to novelists or filmmakers; it is now a crucial element of successful SEO strategies in 2025 and beyond. In an information-saturated landscape, a compelling story can set your brand apart from the competition, fostering an emotional connection with users.

Understanding how your audience consumes content is essential. People are naturally inclined to remember stories more vividly than isolated facts or figures. Research from the Stanford Graduate School of Business highlights that narratives are often more persuasive than statistics alone. Therefore, when creating content, it's important to engage readers emotionally as well as inform them. Instead of simply listing a product's features, consider illustrating how it transformed a customer's life. Sharing testimonials that highlight real-world impact can build trust and relatability.

To effectively weave storytelling into your SEO strategy, begin by understanding your audience's journey. Who are they? What challenges do they face? Mapping out customer personas can provide valuable insights into these questions. With a clear understanding of your audience, you can create content that addresses their pain points through relatable narratives. Take this example, if you sell eco-friendly cleaning products, share the story of a family transitioning to sustainable living—showcasing their struggles and triumphs so readers can see themselves reflected in that experience.

Visual elements significantly enhance storytelling as well. Infographics, videos, and images can add context to your narrative and enrich the text. A case study from a well-known brand illustrates this point: they used video testimonials to share customer stories about their products' effectiveness. The combination of authentic narratives and engaging visuals resulted in increased click-through rates and longer time spent on their pages.

Integrating storytelling into your SEO practices also involves optimizing these narratives for search engines without compromising their essence. Keywords should flow naturally within the story rather than being awkwardly inserted for optimization purposes. For example, if your narrative focuses on overcoming adversity while using your service, incorporate keywords related to those challenges organically throughout the text. This strategy not only aids search engines in understanding your content but also keeps readers engaged.

Social media platforms present excellent opportunities for storytelling as well. Short narratives shared through posts or stories can drive traffic back to your site while building community around your brand. Additionally, encouraging customers to share their own stories related to your products generates authentic content that resonates widely and enhances trustworthiness.

Finally, measuring the impact of storytelling on your SEO efforts is essential for refining your approach. Track engagement metrics such as time on page, bounce rates, and social shares to assess how well your narratives are resonating with audiences. Tools like Google Analytics can offer insights into which stories connect most effectively with your audience, allowing you to adjust future content accordingly.

Storytelling in SEO is not just about crafting engaging narratives; it's about creating meaningful connections that foster loyalty and encourage conversions. By deeply understanding your audience and weaving their experiences into compelling stories, you position your brand not merely as a provider but as an integral part of their journey—transforming passive readers into active participants in a shared narrative. This approach elevates your SEO strategy, making it not only effective but also memorable in an ever-evolving digital landscape where human connection is paramount.

Evergreen vs. Timely Content

Evergreen content and timely content each play a unique role in the SEO landscape, offering distinct benefits that cater to different goals and audience needs. Understanding their differences is crucial for developing a comprehensive content strategy that not only drives traffic but also fosters ongoing engagement.

Evergreen content boasts lasting relevance. This type of content remains applicable regardless of trends or seasonal changes, serving as a reliable source of traffic over time. Examples include how-to guides, tutorials, and foundational articles that address persistent questions or challenges within your niche. Take this example, an article titled "How to Start a Vegetable Garden" continues to attract readers year after year, as gardening remains a popular interest. The key to evergreen content lies in selecting subjects that maintain their significance, providing users with valuable insights that endure.

On the other hand, timely content focuses on current events, trends, or seasonal topics that are relevant for a limited period. Think of blog posts analyzing the latest digital marketing trends or holiday gift guides designed for shoppers during the festive season. These pieces are crafted to capitalize on short-lived spikes in interest and can generate significant traffic when executed effectively. A timely post like "Best SEO Strategies for 2025" may attract immediate attention, particularly if it coincides with industry conferences or discussions taking place at that moment.

To maximize the benefits of both evergreen and timely content, consider developing a balanced content calendar. This approach allows you to plan and publish diverse pieces that serve different purposes while ensuring a consistent flow of material. For example, you might release an evergreen article on "The Basics of SEO" alongside a timely piece about "SEO Trends to Watch This Summer." This strategic mix keeps your audience engaged by catering to varied interests while enhancing your site's overall search engine performance.

When creating evergreen content, prioritize depth and thoroughness. Explore topics through comprehensive research and actionable insights that deliver real value. Incorporating visuals like infographics can enhance understanding and shareability; these elements not only improve user experience but also increase the likelihood of earning backlinks as others reference your work.

Timely content demands agility and responsiveness. Stay attuned to industry news and social media conversations so you can produce relevant pieces quickly. Utilize tools like Google Trends or BuzzSumo to identify what's currently capturing attention in your field. Take this example, if there's a sudden surge in discussions about AI's role in SEO due to recent innovations, promptly create an article analyzing its implications for marketers.

In both types of content, incorporating keywords is essential. For evergreen articles, focus on broad terms that reflect ongoing search behaviors—phrases like "content marketing strategies" or "beginner's guide to SEO." Timely pieces benefit from more specific keywords related to current events; using terms like "2025 digital marketing predictions" helps target users seeking up-to-date information.

Tracking performance is vital for refining your approach over time. Analyze metrics such as organic traffic growth, user engagement rates, and social shares for both evergreen and timely posts. Tools like SEMrush can help assess which keywords drive traffic effectively or reveal new opportunities based on evolving search patterns.

both evergreen and timely content should resonate with your brand's voice and mission while addressing user needs. Achieving the right balance between these two forms enables you to establish authority within your niche while remaining relevant in an ever-changing digital landscape. As you refine your strategy, remember: timeless value cultivates loyal readers, while fresh insights generate immediate interest— together, they create a dynamic approach capable of sustaining engagement over the long term.

Leveraging User-Generated Content

User-generated content (UGC) has become a vital element of contemporary digital marketing, fundamentally changing how brands connect with their audiences. UGC refers to any content —such as reviews, testimonials, social media posts, or videos —created by consumers rather than the brands themselves. By harnessing UGC, companies can build trust and foster a sense of community around their offerings. Given that today's consumers are increasingly skeptical of traditional advertising, authentic voices from fellow users hold significant power.

Incorporating UGC into your SEO strategy presents numerous benefits, starting with enhanced credibility. When potential customers encounter real individuals sharing their experiences with a product or service, it effectively lowers the barriers to purchase. A study by Nielsen revealed that 92% of consumers trust recommendations from people over brands. So, showcasing user testimonials on your website or sharing positive reviews on social media can profoundly influence conversion rates.

A prime example of UGC in action is Airbnb. The platform encourages hosts and guests to share their stories and experiences through photos and reviews. This not only enhances the community feel of Airbnb but also generates organic content that boosts search visibility. Each unique review is indexed by search engines, increasing the diversity of keywords associated with specific properties or destinations. This approach highlights how UGC can organically enhance SEO performance while simultaneously fostering brand loyalty.

To effectively utilize user-generated content, begin by creating spaces for your audience to share their experiences. Social media campaigns that invite customers to post pictures using a specific hashtag can yield valuable content while expanding your reach. Take this example, Coca-Cola's "Share a Coke" campaign encouraged consumers to find bottles labeled with their names and share images online. This initiative engaged users and resulted in millions of pieces of content that amplified the brand's visibility in search results.

Once you've collected UGC, it's crucial to curate and display it thoughtfully on your website. Consider creating dedicated sections for customer testimonials or galleries showcasing user photos related to your products or services. This method allows potential buyers to see real-life examples of how others enjoy what you offer, reinforcing your brand's authenticity.

Incorporating UGC into product pages can also enhance SEO outcomes. For example, placing customer reviews directly beneath product descriptions enriches the content and encourages longer dwell times—an important factor for SEO rankings. To maximize impact, ensure that these reviews naturally incorporate relevant keywords; this aligns with search intent and improves visibility.

Additionally, think about ways to incentivize further UGC creation among your audience. Contests or giveaways that encourage users to submit their experiences can generate a wealth of fresh content while increasing engagement across platforms. Take this example, beauty brands often run campaigns where customers showcase makeup looks created with their products for a chance to win prizes—a mutually beneficial arrangement that sparks excitement and fosters authentic interactions.

Monitoring the effectiveness of user-generated content is essential for ongoing success in this area. Use analytics tools like Google Analytics or social media insights to track engagement rates related to UGC initiatives. Pay attention to metrics such as shares, comments, and clicks on links connected to user-generated posts; this data will help you understand what resonates most with your audience.

As you explore deeper integration of user-generated content into your strategy, remember the importance of cultivating an environment where customers feel valued and heard. Actively engage by responding to comments and sharing user posts on your own channels—this interaction strengthens relationships and encourages more users to contribute their stories.

To wrap things up, embracing user-generated content presents an outstanding opportunity to enhance both engagement and SEO performance in today's digital landscape. By building trust through authentic voices and strategically incorporating UGC into various aspects of your marketing efforts, you position yourself not just as a brand but as part of a vibrant community that prioritizes genuine connections over mere transactions. this approach lays the foundation for long-lasting relationships between brands and consumers—relationships that drive traffic and loyalty over time.

Utilizing Multimedia in Content

Integrating multimedia into your content strategy is no longer just a trend; it has become essential for brands seeking to capture and retain audience attention in 2025. As consumers face an overload of text-heavy information, incorporating diverse formats like videos, infographics, podcasts, and interactive elements can significantly boost engagement. Multimedia provides a dynamic way to present information, enhancing both comprehension and retention—crucial factors in an age where users expect quick and digestible content.

Visual storytelling, through images and videos, greatly enriches the user experience. Studies indicate that people process visuals 60,000 times faster than text, highlighting the importance of incorporating eye-catching graphics into your digital presence. For example, a video tutorial can convey information far more effectively than a lengthy article on the same topic. HubSpot's research underscores this, revealing that adding video to landing pages can increase conversion rates by as much as 80%. This statistic illustrates how leveraging video content not only captivates viewers but also encourages them to take action.

A prime example of effective multimedia integration is Coca-Cola's "Coca-Cola Journey" platform. By employing rich visuals, engaging narratives, and interactive features, they create an immersive experience for users. Their articles frequently include embedded videos, stunning imagery, and infographics that offer insights into the brand's history and initiatives. This approach not only fosters deeper connections with their audience but also boosts their SEO efforts through increased time spent on pages.

When you incorporate multimedia elements into your SEO strategy, it's crucial to optimize these components for search engines. Each image should include descriptive alt text featuring relevant keywords to enhance accessibility and search visibility. For videos, ensure that they come with well-crafted descriptions and tags; after all, YouTube is the second largest search engine worldwide. That's why, optimizing your video content should be a core aspect of your overall strategy.

A practical method is to embed videos on product pages or blog posts where they can provide added value. Creating explainer videos that clearly outline product benefits or user experiences enriches the customer journey while increasing the likelihood of sharing. Additionally, platforms like TikTok or Instagram Reels are excellent for short-form video content that resonates with younger audiences; these platforms not only enhance visibility but also generate valuable backlinks to your primary website.

In addition to visual media, infographics serve as powerful tools for simplifying complex information into easily digestible formats. They enable you to present data insights or processes visually—a particularly effective approach in industries rife with jargon or dense material. Well-designed infographics have a higher chance of being shared across social media platforms or embedded in other websites, naturally creating backlinks that improve SEO.

Podcasts have also emerged as a crucial medium within digital marketing strategies. As listeners increasingly consume audio content during commutes or workouts, launching a podcast series can significantly expand your reach. This format allows for an intimate connection with your audience through storytelling and expert interviews that foster trust and authority in your niche.

Engaging your audience extends beyond simply posting content; tracking its performance is equally important. Tools like Google Analytics can help you monitor metrics such as bounce rates on multimedia-rich pages versus traditional text-based content. Evaluating engagement rates on social media platforms where your multimedia is shared—through likes, shares, and comments—provides invaluable insights into what resonates most with your audience.

To further boost engagement with multimedia elements, consider integrating interactive components like polls or quizzes within your content framework. These tools encourage participation and foster a two-way dialogue between you and your audience—a proven method to enhance retention rates.

As you deepen your integration of multimedia into your marketing efforts, always prioritize high-quality production values that align with your brand messaging. Authenticity shines through well-produced visuals or expertly edited audio tracks; today's consumers can quickly discern when something feels off-brand or hastily produced.

Embracing multimedia goes beyond simply adding embellishments; it necessitates thoughtful consideration of how each element meaningfully contributes to the user experience while simultaneously advancing SEO objectives. By creating diverse content formats tailored to audience preferences and effectively optimizing each piece for search engines, you can position yourself ahead of competitors who remain tethered to written text alone.

mastering multimedia within your strategy paves the way for richer interactions between brands and consumers—fostering loyalty through vibrant engagement while enhancing search visibility across multiple channels over time.

CHAPTER 8: BUILDING AND MAINTAINING BACKLINKS

Understanding the
Importance of Backlinks

B acklinks are the lifeblood of SEO, serving as essential connectors between websites and reflecting credibility and relevance in the digital landscape. Recognizing their importance is only the first step; effectively harnessing their potential requires a strategic approach. As we move into 2025, the backlink landscape is evolving, making it essential for digital marketers to adapt and implement effective strategies that strengthen their link profiles.

The true value of backlinks lies in their capacity to drive organic traffic and enhance search engine rankings. When a reputable site links to your content, it acts as an endorsement, signaling to search engines that your website is a trustworthy source of information. This endorsement can lead to improved rankings in search results, directly influencing visibility and traffic. Take this example, a study by Moz has shown that backlinks remain one of the top three ranking factors in Google's algorithm. This shows the necessity of a robust backlink strategy as part of any comprehensive SEO plan.

However, acquiring quality backlinks is not just about quantity; it's about significance. High-authority backlinks from relevant sites carry much more weight than numerous links from low-quality sources. A single link from an established industry leader can prove more beneficial than dozens from obscure blogs. For example, if you manage a health and wellness blog, securing a backlink from a respected health organization will enhance your credibility far more than links from unrelated websites. This selective approach ensures that your backlink profile remains strong and advantageous for search engine rankings.

One effective method for building quality backlinks is through content marketing. By creating valuable, shareable content—such as in-depth guides, infographics, or original research—you can naturally attract links. When your content offers insights or solutions that others find helpful, they are more likely to reference it in their own articles or resources. BuzzSumo's analysis illustrates this point well: content with visual elements tends to garner more shares and backlinks than text-only pieces. By merging high-quality writing with engaging visuals, you significantly increase your chances of earning those coveted backlinks.

Another strategy involves leveraging relationships within your industry. Networking can lead to guest blogging opportunities where you contribute articles to other sites in exchange for a link back to yours. This not only enhances your backlink profile but also introduces your brand to new audiences. When seeking potential sites for guest posts, ensure they align with your niche and audience interests; this relevance will amplify the impact of the link.

Additionally, exploring newer platforms can yield valuable backlinks. Social media channels play a crucial role in amplifying content reach; when your content is shared widely, it attracts attention from bloggers and journalists looking for sources or references. Crafting shareable snippets or engaging visuals specifically designed for platforms like Instagram or LinkedIn can facilitate this process.

Monitoring your backlink profile is just as important as acquiring them. Regular audits using tools like Ahrefs or SEMrush can help identify which backlinks bolster your SEO efforts and which might be detrimental—such as links from spammy sites that could harm your rankings. If you find low-quality backlinks pointing to your site, take action by disavowing them through Google Search Console to maintain a healthy link profile.

Neglecting your backlink strategy can lead to missed opportunities for growth and visibility. Brands that overlook quality backlink acquisition risk being overshadowed by competitors who effectively utilize this aspect of SEO. Without strong backlinks, even top-notch content may languish unnoticed on the second or third pages of search results.

As you develop your backlink strategy, remember the importance of authenticity and transparency in outreach efforts. Craft personalized messages when reaching out for collaborations or guest posting opportunities; genuine connections often yield more favorable responses than generic requests.

In summary, grasping the significance of backlinks goes far beyond basic acquisition techniques; it involves crafting a holistic approach that aligns with user intent and search engine algorithms. By prioritizing quality over quantity, leveraging industry relationships, and maintaining an active monitoring system, you position yourself favorably within the competitive landscape of SEO in 2025. A robust backlink profile not only enhances visibility but also strengthens your brand's authority —an invaluable asset in navigating today's digital marketplace effectively.

Strategies for Acquiring Quality Links

Backlink acquisition demands a deep understanding of quality over quantity, emphasizing the importance of strategic relationships and value-driven content. To build a strong online presence, it's crucial to develop a diverse link portfolio that aligns with your niche and resonates with your target audience. This approach helps you avoid spammy or irrelevant sources that could damage your credibility. A well-defined backlink strategy lays the groundwork for long-term SEO success.

At the heart of effective backlink strategies is the creation of high-quality, shareable content. Consider producing comprehensive resources that address common challenges within your industry. For example, if you're in the technology sector, you might develop an in-depth white paper or an engaging video tutorial that highlights best practices for emerging technologies. Such resources naturally attract backlinks, as other creators often reference your work in their own articles or videos, thereby extending your influence organically.

A prime example of this strategy is HubSpot's annual "State of Inbound" report. Each year, the extensive data they compile garners numerous backlinks from industry blogs and news sites eager to cite their findings. The takeaway here is to focus on creating content that not only stands out but also becomes a go-to reference for others.

Partnerships can further bolster your link acquisition efforts. Collaborating with influencers or established companies in your industry opens up cross-promotional opportunities. Take this example, co-hosting webinars or engaging in joint research initiatives can lead to mutual backlinks on both parties' platforms. Such partnerships enrich your content offerings and extend your reach to new audiences who may not yet be familiar with your brand.

Additionally, engaging with online communities can yield valuable links. Participating in forums like Reddit or Quora allows you to showcase your expertise while subtly introducing links to relevant content on your site when appropriate. Always prioritize genuine contributions over self-promotion, as adhering to community guidelines cultivates trust and encourages engagement.

Maintaining an active presence on social media channels tailored to your audience is equally important. Sharing snippets of valuable insights from your blog posts or creating shareable infographics can generate buzz around your content, leading to shares that may result in backlinks across various platforms —particularly if those posts resonate with followers who find them useful.

When evaluating potential backlink opportunities, it's essential to assess the domain authority (DA) of the sites you wish to acquire links from. Tools like Moz's Link Explorer enable you to evaluate potential partners based on their DA scores, helping you prioritize outreach efforts towards more credible sources. A focused approach on niche-specific websites amplifies the impact of your backlinks significantly.

Conducting competitor analysis is another effective tactic for identifying backlink sources. Tools like SEMrush allow you to view competitors' profiles and discover where they are acquiring quality links. This information not only reveals missed opportunities but also highlights potential partnerships worth exploring.

Continuously refining your outreach strategy is vital for success. Track metrics such as response rates and conversion rates on outreach emails to understand which messaging resonates most effectively. This insight will help you tailor future efforts for greater impact.

As we navigate the evolving SEO landscape of 2025, adapting these strategies will be essential for maintaining a competitive edge in acquiring quality backlinks that enhance both authority and visibility online. Building meaningful relationships through genuine collaboration and providing exceptional value through quality content will distinguish you in an increasingly crowded digital space.

consistent monitoring and agile adjustments are crucial components of any successful backlink strategy. Regularly auditing existing links using tools like Google Search Console helps maintain a clean profile while ensuring you capitalize on growth opportunities and protect against negative SEO impacts from lower-quality sources.

In this dynamic environment, where algorithms continuously evolve, being proactive rather than reactive will determine how effectively you secure and leverage quality backlinks as we move into 2025—and beyond.

The Dangers of Link Schemes

Link schemes present a serious threat to any SEO strategy aimed at sustainable growth. Engaging in such practices can result in harsh penalties from search engines, which can significantly damage your site's credibility and visibility. To safeguard your efforts, it's crucial to understand the landscape of link schemes and avoid pitfalls that could undermine your hard work.

Common link schemes include buying links, excessive reciprocal linking, and participating in link farms—networks created solely to inflate link counts without regard for relevance or quality. Although these strategies may promise quick ranking boosts, the long-term repercussions are often devastating. Search engines like Google have become increasingly adept at detecting manipulative link-building tactics. For example, the Penguin update targeted sites that engaged in such practices, leading to steep declines in organic traffic.

To illustrate this, imagine an e-commerce website that opts to buy links from a dubious network. Initially, the site might enjoy a surge in rankings due to the rapid accumulation of backlinks. However, when search engines identify the unnatural spike in its link profile, penalties may ensue, pushing the site down below competitors who focus on legitimate link-building efforts. This scenario highlights the necessity of prioritizing quality over quantity when acquiring backlinks.

Instead of resorting to questionable schemes, aim for organic growth through ethical practices that build your domain authority over time. A strong content marketing strategy is essential for attracting genuine backlinks. Producing high-quality articles and resources not only provides value but also establishes your expertise within your niche. Take this example, consider publishing research-backed studies or comprehensive guides that offer insights into industry trends. When others find your content valuable, they are more inclined to reference it in their own work.

Another effective method is to focus on outreach that emphasizes relationship-building rather than transactional exchanges. Instead of simply asking for links, engage with bloggers and influencers in your field by sharing their content or collaborating on mutually beneficial projects. For example, if you manage a health-focused blog, reaching out to fitness coaches or nutritionists for guest posts can generate beneficial links while strengthening community ties.

Monitoring your backlink profile is also vital for maintaining a healthy online presence. Tools like Ahrefs can provide insights into your backlinks and help identify any potentially harmful links pointing to your site. If you find low-quality sources linked to your content, take proactive measures by disavowing those links using Google's disavow tool. This step protects your site from penalties associated with toxic backlinks.

And, staying informed about algorithm updates is essential for avoiding the pitfalls of link schemes. Regularly following SEO news sources such as Search Engine Journal or Moz can keep you updated on changes that might impact link-building strategies.

Quick adaptation ensures compliance with best practices laid out by search engines and mitigates risks associated with outdated techniques.

Engagement within professional communities also fosters organic backlink building. Participating in webinars or industry conferences allows you to network effectively and share valuable insights while naturally linking back to relevant content on your site.

fostering authenticity and providing real value through quality content and ethical outreach will not only enhance your backlink profile but also strengthen your reputation within the digital landscape. Committing to transparency and integrity positions you as a credible source in your industry while steering clear of the risks associated with link schemes—a choice that will yield benefits as search engine algorithms evolve toward more sophisticated assessments of web content quality in 2025 and beyond.

In this rapidly changing environment where securing high-quality backlinks is crucial for success, adhering to ethical principles will distinguish you as an SEO leader dedicated to achieving impactful results without compromising integrity or sustainability.

Analyzing Competitor Backlink Profiles

Analyzing competitor backlink profiles is essential for crafting a strong SEO strategy. By examining the link-building tactics of your competitors, you can uncover opportunities for your own website and refine your methods for acquiring high-quality backlinks. This process begins with identifying your main competitors—those who rank for the same keywords and target the same audience.

To start, leverage tools like Ahrefs or SEMrush to scrutinize your competitors' backlink profiles. Enter their domain names into these tools to generate a comprehensive overview of their backlink sources, anchor text distribution, and overall link health. Take this example, if you operate a digital marketing agency, focus on top-ranking agencies within your niche. Take note of where their backlinks originate—whether from guest posts, industry directories, or social media mentions.

Once you have gathered this information, categorize the backlinks by quality and relevance. A strong backlink should come from a reputable site with high domain authority and be contextually relevant to your content. For example, if a competitor has numerous backlinks from marketing blogs or websites that specialize in digital strategies, it suggests an effective outreach approach that you might want to replicate.

Next, assess the anchor texts used in these backlinks. Are they employing branded terms, exact match keywords, or generic phrases? This understanding can help inform your own anchor text strategy. If you observe that successful competitors frequently use specific keywords as anchor text that you haven't yet targeted, consider incorporating similar phrases into your outreach efforts.

To gain deeper insights, analyze the types of content being linked to on these competitor sites. Are they primarily linking to blog posts, case studies, videos, or infographics? This examination can reveal what type of content resonates well within your niche and attracts links. For example, if you find that comprehensive guides receive more backlinks than other formats, prioritize creating similar high-value content on your own site.

Additionally, conduct a gap analysis between your backlink profile and those of your competitors. Identify which websites link to them but not to you; these represent immediate targets for outreach efforts. Tools like Moz's Link Explorer can effectively visualize these gaps.

Take this example, consider an online fashion retailer analyzing its rival's backlink profile. The analysis might reveal that many links come from popular fashion blogs featuring product reviews and style guides. This insight presents an opportunity: by reaching out to similar bloggers with well-crafted pitches offering collaboration or samples for review purposes, the retailer can establish valuable links that enhance its visibility.

However, it's important to remember that not all backlinks are beneficial; some may originate from less reputable sources that could harm your standing with search engines. Therefore, it's crucial not only to identify potential link sources but also to thoroughly evaluate their quality before pursuing them.

To maintain a healthy backlink profile over time and avoid toxic links—similar considerations apply when analyzing your competitors' profiles as well—periodically check for harmful links pointing toward their sites using tools like Google Search Console or Ahrefs' Site Audit feature. Observing how they manage these links can provide strategies for maintaining link quality on your own site.

To wrap things up, conducting a thorough analysis of competitor backlink profiles equips you with actionable insights that can significantly enhance your link-building strategies. By identifying where competitors excel and leveraging this knowledge creatively in outreach efforts—while focusing on creating high-quality content tailored for targeted audiences —you strategically position yourself within the competitive landscape of SEO. Your commitment to ethical practices combined with insightful analytics lays the groundwork for sustainable growth through authentic connections in the digital space—an approach poised for success in 2025 and beyond.

Relationship Building for Link Acquisition

Building strong relationships is a fundamental pillar of effective link acquisition. While many focus on the technical aspects of link building—such as analyzing competitor profiles or employing specific outreach tactics—the real strength comes from fostering genuine connections with individuals and brands in your industry. Establishing rapport can lead to lasting partnerships that yield not only backlinks but also collaborative opportunities to enhance your overall brand visibility.

Start by engaging with industry influencers and bloggers relevant to your niche. Follow them on social media, interact with their content, and provide thoughtful comments or insights. This initial engagement is crucial; it builds recognition and paves the way for deeper conversations later on. Take this example, if you run a health and wellness blog, commenting on a popular influencer's post about nutrition can open doors for future collaborations, such as guest posts or interviews.

Once you've established some rapport, consider reaching out directly. A personalized message referencing specific work of theirs that you admire can make a strong impression. Instead of sending a generic email asking for a backlink, craft a note highlighting how their recent article influenced your own work. You might suggest ways to collaborate—perhaps co-creating content or sharing insights through an online webinar. This approach demonstrates that you value their expertise and are invested in creating mutual benefits rather than merely seeking links.

Networking at industry events is another effective way to build relationships. Conferences, trade shows, and webinars provide ideal environments for meeting peers face-to-face (or virtually) and exchanging ideas. Attend workshops aligned with your interests, engage actively in discussions, and don't hesitate to introduce yourself. Remember to follow up afterward; an email thanking them for the conversation can solidify the connection and open avenues for future collaboration.

After establishing these connections, consider how they can lead to tangible link acquisition opportunities. For example, if you're connected with an influencer in the travel sector, propose writing a guest post for their site that offers value to their audience—such as travel tips or destination guides—while subtly integrating links back to your own website.

Community involvement is another key aspect of relationship building. Join forums or groups related to your industry where professionals share knowledge and insights. Engaging in these spaces allows you to showcase your expertise while organically identifying potential backlink opportunities through relationship growth. When members recognize your contributions, they may be more inclined to link back to your resources as trusted references.

Take advantage of existing relationships within your network as well. If you've previously collaborated on projects or shared insights with others in your field, reach out about linking opportunities in their content or suggesting cross-promotion strategies. These personal connections can lead to fruitful partnerships because the individuals already trust your work and understand the value you bring.

In local SEO, building relationships is especially important. Partner with local businesses or organizations whose values align with yours; this not only enhances credibility within your community but also opens avenues for local backlinks through sponsorships or joint events. Consider case studies like a local coffee shop partnering with nearby yoga studios to offer discounts; they benefit from each other's audiences while creating natural opportunities for mutual online linking.

However, it's critical to approach relationship-building ethically and thoughtfully. Avoid cold outreach tactics aimed solely at link acquisition without offering something valuable in return; this can damage reputations instead of building them. Instead of viewing connections as transactional, prioritize authenticity in every interaction. This focus will foster trust that leads to reciprocal support over time.

relationship building transforms what could be mere transactional exchanges into genuine partnerships rooted in shared goals and mutual growth. By actively nurturing these connections through authentic engagement—whether online or offline—you position yourself not just as another player seeking links but as a respected member of an industry community that values collaboration and innovation.

By cultivating meaningful relationships, you enhance your link-building strategy while positively contributing to the broader ecosystem of your niche—ensuring sustainable growth for years ahead while adapting to the ever-evolving landscape of SEO practices in 2025 and beyond.

Guest Blogging and its Importance

Guest blogging remains a crucial strategy in the SEO toolkit, serving as both an effective outreach method and a way to enhance domain authority. Although guest blogging has been a staple for years, its significance has grown as digital landscapes evolve and competition increases. For businesses looking to strengthen their online presence, engaging in guest blogging is not merely a tactical choice; it is an essential element of a comprehensive SEO strategy.

When done right, guest blogging allows you to connect with established audiences who may not yet know about your brand. It's akin to receiving an invitation to showcase your expertise on platforms that already attract your target demographic. This approach is particularly beneficial in niche markets, where the right guest post can place your insights directly in front of potential customers seeking solutions related to your products or services. For example, if you operate in the health and wellness sector, contributing to a popular fitness blog can help position you as a thought leader while also driving traffic back to your own site.

To maximize the effectiveness of your guest blogging efforts, start by identifying high-authority websites within your industry that accept guest contributions. Tools like Ahrefs or Moz can help you assess the domain authority of potential sites, allowing you to prioritize platforms that not only attract high traffic but also resonate with your target audience. Once you've compiled a list, reach out with tailored pitches that clearly demonstrate how your content will add value for their readership.

Crafting a compelling pitch is essential. Rather than sending generic emails, personalize each one by referencing specific articles or topics from the site that align with your proposed content. This shows genuine interest and research on your part, increasing the likelihood of a positive response from editors. Take this example, if you're proposing an article on "sustainable living tips," mention previous content they published on related subjects and explain how your piece could offer fresh perspectives.

Once you've secured a guest post opportunity, focus on creating high-quality content that adheres to the host site's guidelines and meets audience expectations. This involves not only delivering valuable insights but also incorporating relevant keywords naturally within the text. Engaging content enhances user experience and encourages readers to share it across social media and other platforms.

Backlinking is another vital aspect of guest blogging. Including strategic links back to your website—whether to relevant blog posts or product pages—can drive organic traffic and improve search rankings. However, balance is key; overly promotional language may alienate readers and editors alike. Ensure that your backlinks are seamlessly integrated within the context of the content and genuinely serve the reader's interests.

Additionally, track the performance of your guest posts using tools like Google Analytics or UTM parameters for precise data collection. Monitoring traffic spikes from specific articles helps you identify which types of content resonate most with audiences and allows you to refine future strategies accordingly.

Guest blogging also fosters relationships within your industry. Engaging with other bloggers and their communities creates networking opportunities that can lead to collaborations, partnerships, or more guest posting chances in the future. It's not just about writing; it's about becoming an integral part of a broader conversation within your niche.

Finally, consider repurposing your guest posts into different formats—such as infographics, podcasts, or videos—to reach diverse audience segments. This strategy amplifies your message while demonstrating adaptability in how you present information. Sharing these formats across multiple platforms can further solidify your brand presence and authority in the market.

In summary, guest blogging transcends merely writing articles for other websites; it's about building connections, increasing visibility, and fostering meaningful engagement in an increasingly crowded digital landscape. By approaching this practice strategically and thoughtfully, you not only elevate your own brand but also contribute significantly to the collective knowledge within your industry—ultimately positioning yourself as an influential voice that others will seek out in the future.

Using Tools for Backlink Analysis

Backlink analysis tools are indispensable allies in crafting a successful SEO strategy. As you explore and refine your backlink profile, these tools offer invaluable insights into the quality, relevance, and effectiveness of the links directing traffic to your website. They enable you to not only track the sources of your backlinks but also evaluate their impact on your domain authority and search rankings.

Ahrefs stands out as one of the most recognized tools for backlink analysis. Its comprehensive features provide a clear view of your backlink profile, allowing you to easily identify which domains link to you, the anchor text employed, and even the estimated traffic generated by those links. Take this example, if a high-authority site references one of your articles on digital marketing strategies, Ahrefs can help you determine whether that link has significantly increased traffic or visibility for that content.

SEMrush is another powerful tool that offers similar functionalities while introducing its own unique features. Its Domain Overview report gives you an instant snapshot of your backlink profile alongside comparisons to competitors. This allows you not only to analyze your own backlinks but also to see which sites are linking to your competitors. Such insights can reveal valuable opportunities for guest blogging or outreach that might otherwise be overlooked.

For those seeking a more detailed examination, Moz's Link Explorer provides in-depth metrics like Page Authority and Domain Authority. Understanding these metrics is vital when evaluating the potential impact of specific backlinks on your SEO efforts. A link from a high Page Authority site carries more weight than one from a lower-authority domain.

Once you have gathered data from these tools, it's essential to assess the quality of the backlinks themselves. Not all backlinks are beneficial; some may originate from spammy or irrelevant sites that could negatively affect your SEO efforts. Tools like Majestic offer metrics such as Trust Flow and Citation Flow, which help gauge the trustworthiness of linking domains. A good practice is to filter out low-quality links and concentrate on those that genuinely add value—particularly links from reputable sources within your industry.

Monitoring changes in your backlink profile over time is equally crucial. Regular audits using these tools can highlight shifts in your backlink landscape—whether due to new acquisitions or lost links—and help you adapt your strategy accordingly. For example, if a significant number of backlinks disappear following an algorithm update or changes in content policies on linked sites, recognizing this trend early allows you to strategize effectively—whether by seeking new partnerships or reinforcing existing ones.

In addition to monitoring current links, these tools facilitate proactive strategies for acquiring new high-quality backlinks through competitive analysis. By examining where competitors are securing their strongest links, you can target similar domains with tailored outreach efforts. If you find that several competitors receive backlinks from a specific industry publication, consider creating compelling content designed specifically for submission to that outlet.

Utilizing UTM parameters when implementing outreach campaigns related to guest blogging or partnership initiatives can enhance your tracking capabilities. By monitoring how much traffic each link generates, you can make informed decisions about where best to invest time and resources in relationship-building.

Finally, while data-driven decisions are essential for developing an effective backlink strategy, personal relationships remain powerful in this realm. Engaging with bloggers and influencers within your industry can create organic opportunities for link acquisition based on mutual respect and shared interests rather than relying solely on cold outreach.

In summary, leveraging backlink analysis tools effectively transforms raw data into actionable insights that elevate your SEO strategies. These tools help ensure you're building a robust network of high-quality links that drive traffic and enhance search engine visibility over time—all while leaving room for creativity and relationship-building initiatives that are fundamental to successful digital marketing endeavors. With a strong foundation established through careful analysis and proactive engagement tactics, you're well-equipped to boost both your site's authority and its presence within an increasingly competitive landscape.

Monitoring and Cleaning Up Bad Links

The quality of your backlink profile plays a crucial role in your website's performance in search engine results. However, it's important to recognize that not all backlinks are equal; some can even undermine your SEO efforts. To maintain a healthy online presence, regularly monitoring and cleaning up poor-quality links is essential. This proactive approach not only protects your site from potential penalties but also enhances its overall authority and credibility.

Start by establishing a baseline of your current backlink profile. Utilize tools like Ahrefs or SEMrush to create a detailed list of the sites linking to you. Focus on metrics such as Domain Authority and Spam Score, which can help you quickly pinpoint potential issues. Take this example, a link from a domain with a high Spam Score may indicate trouble, suggesting that it could have been created through questionable practices.

After compiling this list, assess the context of each backlink. Evaluate the relevance and quality of the referring domains. Are they credible sources within your industry, or do they belong to disreputable networks? Links from low-quality sites can be detrimental to your SEO. If you find links from sites that lack relevance to your content or industry, it's time to take action.

Removing harmful links typically involves reaching out directly to site owners and requesting their removal. While this process can feel daunting, many webmasters appreciate honesty and are willing to help when approached professionally. When crafting your outreach email, keep it concise yet polite, explaining why the link may no longer be beneficial for either party. For example: "I noticed that our site is linked from yours; however, due to recent updates in our content strategy, I believe this link may no longer serve its intended purpose.

If your outreach efforts don't yield results or if you encounter unresponsive webmasters, consider using Google's Disavow Tool as a last resort. This tool allows you to inform Google that certain backlinks should not be considered when assessing your site's authority. However, use this option judiciously —disavowing links without thorough analysis might remove valuable connections along with harmful ones.

In addition to cleaning up existing links, keeping track of newly acquired backlinks over time can help you proactively identify any emerging issues before they escalate. Conducting regular audits—whether monthly or quarterly—will enable you to stay ahead of potential problems by spotting spammy links early on. Over time, this practice will not only protect your site but also enhance its reputation among search engines.

To maintain a robust backlink profile, consider implementing an ongoing monitoring system. Establish alerts for new backlinks so you can evaluate them immediately upon discovery. Tools like Moz's Link Explorer allow you to set up notifications whenever your site gains or loses backlinks, providing timely insights into any changes.

Building relationships within your industry can also mitigate risks associated with bad links. Engaging in community forums or social media platforms enhances visibility and fosters connections with reputable webmasters who may become allies in backlink management efforts. Sharing valuable content or offering guest posts on respected blogs can create opportunities for quality backlinks while nurturing professional relationships that lead to mutual support.

Cleaning up bad links is not just about damage control; it also creates space for more relevant and high-quality backlinks to flourish in your profile. Once you've identified harmful links and taken steps to remove them, focus on acquiring new backlinks from reputable sources within your niche. This proactive strategy ensures that you're not only safeguarding your existing authority but also building upon it with links that genuinely add value.

To wrap things up, actively monitoring and cleaning up bad links is a vital component of a successful SEO strategy. By prioritizing link quality over quantity and implementing systematic approaches for monitoring and disavowing problematic backlinks, you position yourself as a responsible digital marketer committed to ethical practices and long-term success in search engine visibility. As you refine your strategy and strengthen relationships within your industry, you'll enhance both your site's authority and its standing among competitors in the ever-evolving digital landscape.

Future Trends in Link Building

The landscape of link building is evolving rapidly, influenced by changes in search engine algorithms and the growing sophistication of user behavior. To remain competitive, it's essential to understand emerging trends that will not only keep your strategies relevant but also enhance your website's position in search rankings.

One significant trend is the move toward holistic and context-driven backlink strategies. Search engines are becoming increasingly skilled at assessing links based on their relevance and quality, rather than merely their quantity. This shift underscores the importance of obtaining backlinks from authoritative sites within your niche, which can greatly enhance your SEO performance. Conversely, links from unrelated or low-quality sources can be detrimental. Therefore, building relationships with industry influencers, thought leaders, and niche-specific sites is crucial. These connections can foster organic backlink growth through collaboration and content sharing.

For example, consider a small e-commerce business that specializes in eco-friendly products. By engaging with sustainability bloggers and participating in forums focused on environmental issues, this business could earn backlinks from credible sources that align with its brand values. Such partnerships not only improve link quality but also increase visibility among target audiences who prioritize eco-conscious practices.

Another trend shaping link building is the central role of

content marketing in acquiring high-quality backlinks. Creating shareable content—such as infographics, comprehensive guides, or interactive tools—can attract attention from media outlets and bloggers seeking authoritative resources to reference. Take this example, if our hypothetical e-commerce business publishes an extensive guide on sustainable living, it could pique the interest of websites dedicated to green living, potentially resulting in valuable backlinks from relevant sources.

As AI technology continues to advance, utilizing tools that employ machine learning for link analysis will become increasingly important. These sophisticated tools can identify patterns within backlink profiles and highlight opportunities for improvement by examining competitors' linking strategies. This helps marketers to refine their approaches based on insights about which types of content or platforms yield the best results for acquiring links in their specific market segment.

The rise of video content also plays a crucial role in future link building strategies. With platforms like YouTube leading online engagement, producing compelling video content can lead to increased shares and backlinks from diverse channels. For example, a how-to video showcasing the use of eco-friendly products not only provides value but may also inspire viewers to link back to the source out of appreciation for the informative material.

Local SEO practices are expected to significantly influence link building strategies as businesses seek deeper connections with their local audiences. Securing backlinks from local news websites and community blogs will become increasingly important. A regional brand could gain substantial benefits from being featured in a local magazine or mentioned in city blogs highlighting neighborhood activities.

Additionally, an emphasis on ethical SEO practices will push brands toward greater transparency regarding their backlinking efforts. As awareness around online authenticity grows among users and search engines alike, ensuring that all backlink acquisitions are legitimate and ethically sourced will be essential. Transparency builds trust—not just with search engines but also with your audience—reinforcing your brand's credibility and authority.

Finally, staying informed about regulatory changes related to data privacy is critical when developing outreach strategies that involve personal data or target specific demographics for links. Understanding laws such as GDPR is vital since they impact how marketers approach linking requests and campaigns reliant on user data.

In summary, embracing the future of link building requires an adaptable mindset focused on quality over quantity. By nurturing meaningful relationships within your industry ecosystem, leveraging innovative content strategies aligned with audience interests, employing advanced analytical tools powered by AI, and adhering to ethical standards regarding transparency and privacy regulations—you'll not only stay ahead of trends but also create a sustainable framework that enhances both your site's authority and visibility in an increasingly competitive digital marketplace.

CHAPTER 9: LOCAL SEO TACTICS FOR HYPERLOCAL RESULTS

The Rise of Local SEO

The digital marketing landscape has transformed dramatically in recent years, with local SEO becoming a vital component for businesses looking to succeed in their markets. As consumers increasingly rely on search engines to discover nearby services and products, optimizing for local search has become essential. This trend is not a passing fad; it represents a strategic necessity that can significantly boost visibility and customer engagement.

Several factors contribute to the rise of local SEO, particularly the surge in mobile device usage and the growing reliance on location-based services. Today, when someone searches for "best coffee shop near me," they anticipate immediate and relevant results. This expectation compels businesses to tailor their online presence for local audiences, creating a digital footprint that resonates within the community while maximizing exposure through targeted search strategies.

A practical example of this is small businesses utilizing Google My Business (GMB). Claiming and optimizing a GMB listing is one of the most effective ways to enhance local visibility. Take this example, consider a new bakery in town. By meticulously filling out their GMB profile—complete with enticing photos of pastries, updated hours, and direct ordering links—they not only improve their chances of appearing in local search results but also create an inviting first impression that encourages foot traffic.

In addition to GMB, local citations—mentions of your business across various online directories—are crucial for establishing credibility and authority within your community. A well-structured citation strategy includes not only traditional directories like Yelp or Yellow Pages but also niche-specific platforms relevant to your industry. For example, if our bakery is featured on food blogs or forums discussing local eateries, it enhances their visibility further while building trust through contextual relevance.

Reviews are another key element of local SEO that should not be overlooked. They act as modern-day word-of-mouth referrals that significantly influence consumer decisions. A business with numerous positive reviews will not only rank higher but also attract more customers due to social proof. Encouraging satisfied customers to leave reviews on platforms like Google or Yelp can dramatically boost visibility and credibility.

Consider this scenario: A plumbing service in Austin actively seeks reviews after each job completion. Over time, they accumulate numerous five-star ratings accompanied by detailed testimonials about their quality work. This practice not only improves their ranking for relevant keywords but also offers potential customers valuable insights into the service experience, ultimately driving more business.

The integration of voice search further underscores the

importance of local SEO strategies. With smart speakers and mobile voice assistants becoming commonplace, users increasingly rely on voice queries like "Where's the closest gas station?" Optimizing for these conversational phrases requires businesses to rethink their keyword strategies, focusing on natural language processing and localized content that aligns with everyday speech.

Additionally, leveraging location-based content through blog posts or community engagement initiatives can solidify a business's position as a local authority. For example, an outdoor gear store might create articles about regional hiking trails or sponsor local events such as cleanup drives—initiatives that foster community goodwill while organically attracting backlinks from relevant sites.

Crucially, website optimization for local searches cannot be overlooked. Ensuring your site is mobile-friendly is essential since many users conduct searches while on the go. And, incorporating location-based keywords naturally throughout your site content enhances its relevance in search engine algorithms.

As you explore local SEO practices more deeply, it becomes clear that this discipline extends beyond simply ranking high on search engines; it focuses on building genuine connections with your community and establishing your brand as a trusted resource within it. Implementing effective local SEO strategies requires consistent effort and adaptation to changing user behaviors and technological advancements but can yield significant returns when executed well.

To wrap things up, embracing the rise of local SEO strategically positions businesses in an increasingly competitive landscape where personalization and relevance are key drivers of success. By utilizing tools such as Google My Business, actively managing online reviews, creating location-specific content, and ensuring a seamless user experience—all these elements come together to form a powerful strategy that enhances brand visibility while strengthening customer relationships at the grassroots level.

Setting Up Google My Business

Claiming and optimizing your Google My Business (GMB) listing is one of the most effective ways for local businesses to boost their visibility. This free tool from Google allows you to manage your online presence across platforms like Search and Maps, making it easier for potential customers to find essential information about your business.

To get started, visit the Google My Business website and click on "Manage now." You'll be prompted to enter your business name. If your business is already listed in Google's database, you can claim it; if not, you can create a new entry. This step is crucial, as it lays the groundwork for how your business will appear in search results. Remember to use the exact name as it appears in real life—consistency is vital for local SEO.

Once your listing is established, it's important to provide comprehensive details about your business. Fill out every section of your profile, including your address, phone number, website URL, and hours of operation. Make sure the address matches how it appears on other platforms and directories to avoid confusing both search engines and users.

Selecting appropriate categories for your business is another critical aspect of optimization. Categories help Google understand the services or products you offer, enabling them to match your listing with relevant searches. For example, if you operate a bakery, ensure "Bakery" is one of your primary categories. You might also consider adding categories like "Coffee Shop" or "Café" if they apply.

Visual content is essential for capturing the attention of potential customers. High-quality images of your products or services not only showcase what you offer but also improve engagement on your listing. According to a study by Google, businesses with photos receive 42% more requests for directions and 35% more click-throughs to their websites than those without. Regularly updating these images—such as featuring seasonal offerings or special events—will keep your profile looking fresh and inviting.

Encouraging customer reviews is another cornerstone of an effective GMB strategy. After providing a service or selling a product, invite satisfied customers to leave feedback on your profile. Responding to reviews—both positive and negative—shows that you value customer input and are engaged with your audience. Take this example, when addressing negative reviews, maintain an empathetic tone and offer solutions; this not only reflects strong customer service skills but also builds trust with potential clients who may read these interactions.

Utilizing posts on GMB can also help keep customers informed about promotions or upcoming events directly in the search results. These posts allow you to share updates such as special discounts or new menu items, engaging users right at their decision-making moment.

Consider a local florist that regularly updates their GMB profile with posts about seasonal arrangements for holidays like Valentine's Day or Mother's Day. By sharing enticing visuals along with brief descriptions or special offers through GMB posts, they can attract more foot traffic during peak seasons.

Implementing a Q&A section on GMB can further enhance customer experience, as many users have common questions before visiting a location (e.g., "Do you offer gluten-free options?"). Proactively answering these inquiries saves time for both parties and improves customer satisfaction.

Finally, maintaining accuracy over time is essential for optimal GMB presence. If anything changes—whether it's adjusting hours due to holiday schedules or relocating entirely—be sure to update these details promptly across all platforms where you're listed.

In summary, effectively setting up Google My Business requires thoroughness—from claiming your listing to consistently maintaining accurate information and engaging content over time. As competition for visibility in local searches grows, leveraging GMB becomes crucial not just for attracting clicks but also for fostering community connections that drive foot traffic and establish brand loyalty. Each effort made here enhances both search engine visibility and trust within the community— an advantage that no modern business should overlook.

Local Keyword Research Techniques

Local keyword research is the foundation of a successful local SEO strategy. By identifying and leveraging keywords that resonate with your target audience in your specific geographic area, you can significantly enhance your online visibility. This process begins with understanding the unique characteristics of local search behavior, which often diverges from broader keyword strategies.

To kick off your research, utilize tools like Google Keyword Planner or Ubersuggest to discover potential local keywords. Start by entering terms relevant to your business along with your city or region, then analyze the results. For example, if you own a yoga studio in Austin, you might come across keywords such as "yoga classes in Austin" or "best yoga studio Austin." It's essential to pay attention to search volume and competition levels, as this data will help you choose keywords that balance frequency of search with manageable competition.

Long-tail keywords are particularly beneficial for local SEO. These phrases typically incorporate specific details about your service or product along with the location, making them more likely to convert visitors into customers. Instead of simply targeting "yoga," consider longer phrases like "affordable yoga classes near me" or "beginner yoga classes in South Austin." Such queries indicate a focused intent from users who are eager to find businesses that cater to their specific needs.

Another effective technique is to explore related searches on

Google. After entering a keyword in the search bar, scroll down to see the "searches related to" section at the bottom of the page. This feature can provide valuable insights into what local customers are seeking. By analyzing these related searches, you can uncover new opportunities and refine your keyword strategy even further.

Social media platforms also offer a wealth of information on local trends and discussions. Sites like Facebook and Nextdoor can reveal what potential customers are saying about products or services similar to yours in the area. Participating in local community groups not only provides insights but also helps foster relationships that may lead to organic traffic and referrals.

Customer feedback can be a rich source for guiding your keyword research as well. Analyzing reviews on platforms such as Yelp or Google Reviews may reveal common phrases or questions that customers use when describing their experiences. Take this example, if numerous reviews highlight terms like "eco-friendly" alongside "flower shop," it signals strong local interest that should be integrated into your keyword strategy—such as using "eco-friendly flower delivery in [City]."

Geotagging your content further enhances its relevance in local searches. By embedding geographical data into images on your website or naturally incorporating city names within blog posts, you signal to search engines your focus on location-specific content. If you're a restaurant owner blogging about new menu items, mentioning "new dishes available at [Your Restaurant Name] in [City]" not only optimizes for keywords but also provides geographic context for your content.

Monitoring competitors' keyword strategies can also yield valuable insights. Tools like SEMrush allow you to analyze which keywords drive traffic to competitor sites within your locality. If their focus areas align with yours yet show higher ranking potential, this information can help inform adjustments to your own strategy.

Incorporating local SEO into existing content is equally important. Take this example, if you've previously written an article about the health benefits of yoga without emphasizing its location-based aspects, updating it could attract more localized traffic. Including details about community events or partnerships strengthens connections with both users and search engines.

Finally, tracking performance is crucial after implementing these strategies. Use analytics tools to evaluate how well specific keywords perform over time—pay attention to organic traffic sources and conversion rates linked directly back to those keywords. Be prepared to make adjustments based on data insights; if certain long-tail keywords yield high engagement while others falter, shifting focus can optimize future efforts.

Effective local keyword research blends an understanding of user intent with community engagement. By combining analytical approaches with genuine connection-building strategies, you can solidify your position within the market landscape. Each step taken enhances visibility while aligning closely with consumer expectations, ultimately fostering growth in both online presence and physical patronage as users discover and engage with your business more frequently through tailored local search efforts.

Importance of Reviews and Ratings

In today's digital landscape, reviews and ratings have transformed from simple customer feedback into powerful tools that can significantly impact a business's online presence. They provide more than just social proof; they actively shape consumer decisions and are crucial for local search rankings. Understanding their importance is vital for anyone looking to enhance their local SEO strategy.

When potential customers search for products or services, they increasingly depend on reviews to inform their choices. For example, imagine two restaurants in the same neighborhood offering similar cuisines and price points. If one has an average rating of 3 stars from 50 reviews, while the other boasts a 4.5-star rating with 200 reviews, it's evident which option consumers are likely to prefer. Search engines recognize this behavior, prioritizing businesses with higher ratings and larger review volumes in local search results.

To cultivate a strong online reputation, encouraging customers to leave reviews is essential. One effective approach is to ask for feedback after a purchase or service. Take this example, if you own a landscaping business, consider following up with clients via email shortly after completing a project. A message like, "We hope you're enjoying your new garden! If you have a moment, we'd greatly appreciate your feedback on our services," can encourage satisfied customers to share their experiences online.

Leveraging platforms like Google My Business (GMB) can further enhance your visibility. GMB enables businesses to manage their online presence across Google, including Search and Maps. By ensuring that your GMB listing is complete—with accurate information, engaging images, and relevant posts—you increase your chances of appearing prominently in local search results. Actively managing customer interactions on GMB not only boosts visibility but also demonstrates your commitment to customer satisfaction.

Proactively addressing negative reviews is another critical aspect of maintaining a positive online reputation. Ignoring criticism can damage your brand image and deter potential customers from engaging with your business. Instead, respond thoughtfully and professionally to any negative feedback you receive. Take this example, if a reviewer mentions poor service during a busy period at your café, acknowledge their experience and express a willingness to improve: "Thank you for your feedback! We're sorry that our service didn't meet expectations during your visit—we appreciate you bringing this to our attention."

The frequency of reviews is just as important as their quality; consistently accumulating positive feedback signals credibility to both search engines and consumers alike. Implementing strategies such as loyalty programs or offering small incentives for leaving reviews can help maintain a steady flow of fresh content. For example, a bakery might offer discounts on future purchases when customers share their experiences online—creating an ongoing dialogue that encourages repeat visits.

Additionally, the content of the reviews themselves can provide valuable insights into consumer preferences and behavior patterns. Analyzing keywords commonly used in positive comments allows businesses to identify what resonates with customers most—whether it's product quality or exceptional customer service—and refine marketing strategies accordingly. Take this example, if multiple reviewers highlight the "friendly staff" at an auto repair shop, incorporating phrases that emphasize outstanding customer service into website content can align messaging with consumer expectations.

Visual content also plays an increasingly significant role in the effectiveness of reviews. Encouraging customers to share images alongside their written feedback can enhance engagement; photos serve as authentic endorsements that validate the experiences shared by others. A fitness center could promote user-generated content by running campaigns that showcase transformations or community events where members document their progress—amplifying word-of-mouth marketing through visuals.

Integrating user-generated content into marketing efforts not only strengthens credibility but also fosters community connections among customers. Prominently featuring testimonials on landing pages or social media channels creates an inviting atmosphere where prospective clients feel encouraged to engage with existing clientele's experiences.

tracking the impact of reviews on SEO performance is crucial for continuous improvement. Monitoring metrics such as search rankings in relation to changes in review volume provides insights into how consumer perceptions affect online visibility. Tools like BrightLocal offer valuable analytics regarding review generation trends in local markets—enabling businesses to make strategic adjustments based on real-time data.

Incorporating effective review management practices into local SEO strategies isn't just beneficial; it's essential for establishing a competitive edge in crowded markets. As consumers become more discerning about where they spend their money, nurturing positive relationships through genuine engagement becomes not only advantageous but critical for long-term success in digital marketing landscapes where reputation truly matters most.

Local Link Building Strategies

Creating a robust local link profile is a vital element of any successful local SEO strategy. Unlike traditional link building, which often prioritizes authority and relevance across broader niches, local link building focuses on geographic proximity and community engagement. This targeted approach not only enhances your search engine rankings but also strengthens your business's reputation within the local community.

To begin, identify relevant local websites and organizations that can offer valuable backlinks. Local news outlets, community blogs, chambers of commerce, and educational institutions are excellent starting points. Take this example, if you own a boutique in a small town, consider reaching out to the local newspaper to feature an article about your grand opening. This not only provides exposure but also results in a valuable backlink. Additionally, offering to write a guest post on fashion trends for a community blog can help establish your authority while linking back to your site.

Participating in local events or sponsorships is another effective strategy. Businesses that engage with their communities often earn backlinks from event pages or announcements. If you sponsor a local sports team or charity event, make sure your business name and website are included in promotional materials that are frequently published online. This practice not only enhances your credibility but can also generate organic traffic from individuals interested in the event.

Collaborating with other local businesses can further enhance your link-building efforts. Joint marketing initiatives can create mutual linking opportunities. For example, if you're a florist partnering with a wedding planner, consider co-hosting a workshop where both businesses are mentioned online with links to each other's sites. These collaborations strengthen community ties and generate relevant content that search engines value.

Social media plays an important role in boosting your local link profile as well. Engaging posts that highlight partnerships or community involvement can attract the attention of influencers or bloggers in your area who might share your content or link back to it on their platforms. Take this example, a well-crafted Instagram story showcasing your participation in a charity event could lead to mentions by attendees with larger followings.

While quality is crucial, consistency is equally important in local link-building strategies. Regularly publishing press releases about new products, services, or events keeps your business top-of-mind for journalists and bloggers seeking fresh content ideas. For example, if you launch an environmentally friendly product line at your store, crafting an engaging press release about this initiative could attract media coverage—resulting in backlinks from various news outlets.

Engaging with online directories specific to your area is another way to increase visibility while enhancing link-building efforts. Ensure that your listings are complete and up-to-date across platforms like Yelp or TripAdvisor, as these resources are frequently consulted by consumers looking for recommendations.

Monitoring and evaluating the effectiveness of these strategies is essential for growth and optimization. Tools like Moz or Ahrefs can provide insights into the health of your backlink profile and help identify potential opportunities based on competitors' strategies. Tracking metrics such as referral traffic from these links offers tangible evidence of what's working best.

Creating valuable content that resonates with the local audience also strengthens link-building efforts. Consider producing resources like neighborhood guides or industry-specific insights tailored for residents. For example, if you run a bakery known for its artisanal bread-making techniques, writing an informative blog post about baking tips specific to regional tastes could attract attention from food bloggers seeking fresh angles—resulting in meaningful backlinks.

nurturing relationships within the community goes beyond just acquiring links; it fosters trust and loyalty among customers who appreciate businesses committed to giving back locally—a sentiment reflected both online and offline.

By thoughtfully implementing these localized link-building strategies consistently—not as isolated campaigns but as integral parts of daily operations—you'll cultivate not just links but lasting relationships that enhance brand visibility while demonstrating a commitment to community involvement—both critical elements for success in today's competitive digital landscape.

Leveraging Local Directories

Local directories have become essential tools for businesses looking to strengthen their online presence, especially within their communities. These platforms not only increase visibility but also build trust among local customers. When individuals search for products or services, they frequently turn to well-known directories like Yelp, Yellow Pages, and Google My

Business (GMB). Claiming and optimizing your listings on these platforms is a critical component of a successful local SEO strategy.

To begin, create or claim your business listing on Google My Business. This foundational step gives you control over how your business appears in local search results. An optimized GMB profile should include key information such as your business name, address, phone number (NAP), hours of operation, website link, and high-quality images. Additionally, keeping your profile active with regular updates about promotions or events can make it more engaging. For example, if you're running a limited-time offer on a popular product or service, highlighting it on your GMB profile can drive more foot traffic and online inquiries.

In addition to Google My Business, other local directories can further enhance your visibility. Platforms like Yelp allow customers to leave reviews and ratings, which significantly influence the decisions of potential clients. A business with numerous positive reviews tends to be viewed as more trustworthy compared to those lacking feedback. To encourage satisfied customers to share their experiences, consider sending follow-up emails after service delivery or offering incentives for honest reviews.

Maintaining consistency across multiple directory listings is crucial. Ensure that your NAP information remains uniform across all platforms; discrepancies can confuse potential customers and hinder search engine algorithms from effectively ranking your business. Tools like Moz Local or BrightLocal can help streamline this process by scanning various directories for inconsistencies and suggesting necessary corrections.

Another advantage of utilizing local directories is the opportunity to generate backlinks, which are vital for improving domain authority and search rankings. High-quality backlinks from reputable sites signal credibility to search engines. Many local directories allow businesses to include a link back to their website in their profiles; this simple action can enhance both traffic and SEO performance.

Effectively utilizing categories within these directories is equally important. Most platforms allow businesses to select relevant categories that best describe their offerings. Choosing the right categories increases the likelihood of appearing in relevant searches when users look for specific services in your area. Take this example, if you operate a coffee shop that also sells baked goods, listing yourself under both "Cafes" and "Bakeries" helps you reach a broader audience.

Engaging with customer queries through directory listings adds another layer of interaction that strengthens community ties and fosters brand loyalty. Timely responses to questions or reviews on platforms like Yelp or Facebook Business Pages reflect positively on your customer service ethos—an essential aspect of local marketing.

Lastly, consider incorporating local events into your directory profiles. If you're participating in community events or hosting workshops at your location, make sure to highlight them prominently in your listings. This not only boosts engagement but also positions you as an active member of the community— a trait many consumers prioritize when deciding where to spend their money.

Leveraging local directories goes beyond mere presence; it requires a strategic approach to how you present your business within these spaces. The goal is not just visibility but also cultivating relationships with local customers who are searching for services like yours—ready to engage with businesses that stand out through quality presentation and consistent interaction. By focusing on these aspects of your online presence within local directories, you'll strengthen your position in the community while significantly enhancing your overall SEO efforts.

Optimizing for Voice Searches

Voice search has evolved from a futuristic idea into a fundamental aspect of how consumers interact with technology. The rise of smart speakers, smartphones, and voice-enabled devices has made optimizing for voice search essential for businesses aiming to stay competitive in today's digital landscape. Unlike traditional text-based searches, voice queries tend to be longer and more conversational, prompting a need to rethink keyword strategies and content creation to better reflect natural speech patterns.

To effectively optimize for voice search, it's important to grasp the characteristics of voice queries. These inquiries often use everyday language, with users asking complete questions rather than inputting fragmented keywords. For example, instead of searching for "best pizza NYC," a voice search might be phrased as, "What's the best pizza place near me?" This shift means businesses should focus on long-tail keywords that align with how people naturally speak. Utilizing tools like AnswerThePublic or Google's "People also ask" feature can help identify common questions in your industry. By integrating these questions into your content, you increase your chances of appearing in voice search results.

Consider also the context in which voice searches are made. Many users employ voice commands while multitasking or on the move, often seeking quick answers. This urgency highlights the importance of concise yet informative content that directly addresses common queries. Structuring your content in a FAQ format can be particularly beneficial. For example, if you run a local bakery, creating a "Frequently Asked Questions" section that answers common inquiries like "What are your opening hours?" or "Do you offer gluten-free options?" not only optimizes for voice search but also enhances user experience.

Local optimization is another crucial aspect to consider. Since voice searches frequently have local intent, keeping your business information current and accessible across platforms like Google My Business is vital. Incorporating location-based keywords into your content can improve relevance when users conduct local searches. Phrases such as "best bakery in [Your City]" or "coffee shops near [Your Neighborhood]" can significantly boost visibility among nearby customers seeking immediate solutions.

Technical elements also play a key role in optimizing for voice search. Websites that load quickly and are mobile-friendly enhance user experience, which can positively impact search rankings. Google's algorithms prioritize mobile responsiveness and speed; thus, ensuring your website performs well on mobile devices is essential for catering to voice search users who may be looking for information quickly.

Incorporating schema markup can provide an additional advantage in optimizing for voice search. This structured data helps search engines better understand your content's context and can lead to rich snippets—enhanced listings that offer immediate information at a glance. Implementing schema markup for FAQs or local business details makes it easier for search engines to retrieve relevant information for voice queries.

Engaging with user-generated content further amplifies your visibility in voice search results. Encouraging customers to leave reviews and feedback not only builds trust but also generates conversational phrases associated with your brand. If customers frequently mention specific products or services in their reviews using natural language, those phrases may surface in relevant searches.

Finally, staying informed about technological advancements is crucial as the landscape continues to evolve rapidly. Voice assistants are increasingly leveraging AI and machine learning to deliver personalized results based on user behavior and preferences. Keeping up with these changes can help you refine your strategies over time and maintain relevance as user expectations shift.

Optimizing for voice search requires a comprehensive approach that encompasses keyword strategy, technical readiness, localized content, and customer engagement. As more consumers adopt this hands-free searching method, businesses that adapt will position themselves advantageously within their markets—becoming leaders in this new era of SEO. The journey involves continuous learning and adaptation; taking proactive steps now will yield significant rewards as reliance on voice technology becomes even more integrated into daily life.

NAP Consistency and Its Impact

Maintaining consistency in your Name, Address, and Phone Number (NAP) across online platforms is a critical yet often overlooked aspect of local SEO. For businesses looking to thrive in their communities, presenting clear and uniform information online is essential. A consistent NAP not only enhances the user experience but also signals trustworthiness to search engines, which can improve visibility in local search results.

To achieve NAP consistency, ensure that your business name, address, and phone number are identical across all listings, including Google My Business, Yelp, Facebook, and industry-specific directories. For example, if your business is listed as "Joe's Pizza" on Google but appears as "Joe's Pizzeria" on Yelp, these discrepancies can confuse potential customers and damage your credibility. Search engines prioritize consistent information when assessing the relevance of a business to local searches; inconsistencies can result in lower rankings.

When establishing your NAP, pay close attention to detail. Use a uniform format for addresses—steer clear of variations like "St." versus "Street." If your business operates multiple locations, ensure that each has its own dedicated listing with accurate information. Additionally, make sure phone numbers are clickable on mobile devices; this small adjustment can significantly enhance user experience.

To effectively monitor NAP consistency, consider utilizing tools specifically designed for local SEO management. Services such as Moz Local or BrightLocal can automate tracking across various directories. These platforms provide insights into how your business appears online and alert you to any inconsistencies that require correction. Regular audits should be standard practice; even minor changes—like relocating offices—necessitate updates across all platforms to maintain integrity.

The implications of NAP consistency extend beyond just improving search engine rankings. A uniform online presence fosters customer trust by delivering a seamless experience as they engage with your brand through different channels. Take this example, if someone discovers your business via a mobile search but encounters conflicting information on social media or review sites, they may decide against visiting altogether. This potential loss of traffic underscores the importance of accurate listings.

Engaging with customer reviews also contributes to the broader context of NAP consistency. Customers often mention specific details about their experiences that can either affirm or challenge the accuracy of your listings. Encouraging satisfied clients to leave positive feedback while promptly addressing negative reviews can enhance your online reputation and provide valuable insights into how users perceive your brand.

Also, integrating schema markup into your website can improve how search engines interpret your NAP data. Schema markup adds context for search engines regarding critical information about your business. When implemented correctly, it increases the likelihood of appearing in rich snippets—enhanced search results that display relevant information directly on the search page.

As the digital landscape evolves towards more localized searches driven by mobile devices and AI technologies, maintaining NAP consistency will be increasingly vital for businesses seeking a competitive edge in their areas. Adopting practices that ensure accuracy across all platforms isn't just about compliance; it's an investment in customer satisfaction and brand reliability.

establishing a solid foundation for NAP is a straightforward yet powerful strategy that drives visibility and engagement. By ensuring users find consistent information at every turn—from social media pages to review sites—you lay the groundwork for building strong relationships within your community and improving overall SEO performance. As local searches continue to rise and consumer behavior shifts toward immediate solutions found through smartphones and voice queries alike, those who prioritize NAP consistency will be well-positioned for success both now and in the future.

Event-Based Local SEO Techniques

Event-based local SEO techniques harness the unique opportunities offered by community events to boost visibility and engagement for local businesses. By tapping into the heightened interest and search activity surrounding these events, businesses can strategically position themselves in relevant searches. Integrating event-based content into your SEO strategy can lead to substantial benefits.

The first step is identifying key events in your area, which may include seasonal festivals, sports games, or local charity drives. Take this example, if you own a bakery, participating in or sponsoring a local food festival can create excitement and attract new customers. Optimizing your online presence around these occasions is essential; this involves crafting content that resonates with the themes and audiences associated with the events.

To effectively engage potential customers during an event, consider creating dedicated landing pages that highlight your participation or any promotions tied to the occasion. If your business is involved in a holiday market, for example, develop a page showcasing special offers, event details, and engaging content such as blog posts or videos that give attendees a preview of what to expect. Incorporating location-based keywords in your titles and meta descriptions—like "Holiday Market at [Location]" or "Join Us at [Event Name]"—will help ensure search engines recognize the relevance of your content.

Social media platforms are also invaluable for amplifying event-related content. Use channels like Facebook and Instagram to share updates leading up to the event, encouraging user engagement through contests or giveaways. Posting live updates during the event allows you to interact with attendees in real-time while attracting those who may not be present but discover your business through social media interactions.

Collaborating with other local businesses involved in the same event is another effective strategy. By co-promoting activities, you can extend your reach beyond your usual audience while fostering community relationships that benefit everyone involved. For example, a local coffee shop could partner with nearby artisans at a craft fair; cross-promoting each other's offerings builds goodwill within the community and enhances visibility across multiple customer bases.

Email marketing is also crucial in this context. If you have an existing customer base subscribed to your newsletter, send out targeted emails before events detailing how they can engage with you—be it through exclusive discounts or special giveaways for email subscribers who visit your booth. Personalization is key; segmenting your audience based on previous interactions ensures that relevant messaging reaches those most likely to respond.

Post-event analysis is equally important. After an event concludes, gather data on engagement metrics such as foot traffic at your booth, social media interactions, and changes in website traffic related to event-specific content. This information provides valuable insights into what worked well and what could be improved for future events.

Incorporating user-generated content (UGC) after an event can further enhance your strategy. Encourage attendees to share their experiences online—whether through photos taken at your booth or testimonials about products they purchased—and feature this UGC on your website or social media platforms. This authentic content not only fosters community but also builds credibility among potential customers exploring their options online.

As search engines continue to refine algorithms that prioritize local relevance and engagement metrics—particularly with mobile-first indexing—event-based SEO techniques will become increasingly vital for driving both foot traffic and online visibility within communities. Businesses that actively participate in local events while optimizing their digital presence accordingly will be better positioned against competitors who overlook these opportunities.

In summary, effectively implementing event-based local SEO techniques requires strategic planning coupled with active participation in the community landscape where you operate. Embracing this proactive approach cultivates connections between brands and consumers while capitalizing on timely opportunities that align with consumer interests—ultimately enhancing both engagement levels and SEO performance over time.

CHAPTER 10:
MEASURING AND
ANALYZING SEO
PERFORMANCE

Overview of SEO Metrics

U nderstanding SEO metrics is crucial for professionals navigating the complexities of search engine optimization. These metrics act as a compass, guiding decisions and strategies based on data rather than assumptions. By familiarizing themselves with key performance indicators (KPIs), marketers can evaluate their efforts, optimize campaigns, and ultimately achieve better results.

One foundational metric to consider is organic traffic, which represents the number of visitors arriving at your site through unpaid search results. Tracking this figure over time offers valuable insights into the effectiveness of your SEO strategies. Take this example, if a recent content update coincides with a spike in organic traffic, it suggests that your adjustments were successful. Tools like Google Analytics provide detailed reports that segment this traffic by source, allowing for a deeper understanding of which keywords and pages are driving visits.

Another critical metric is keyword rankings. Monitoring where your website stands for targeted keywords helps assess the success of your optimization efforts. A decline in rankings for specific terms may indicate that competitors are gaining ground or that changes in search engine algorithms have affected visibility. Regularly checking these rankings—using tools like SEMrush or Ahrefs—enables you to adjust your strategy promptly to maintain or regain visibility.

Bounce rate is also essential for gauging user engagement. A high bounce rate may suggest that visitors aren't finding what they expected on your site, prompting them to leave quickly. If users frequently exit after viewing only one page, it's worth investigating whether your content aligns with their intent or if navigation barriers hinder further exploration. Tools like Hotjar can provide heatmaps that reveal where users click or scroll, helping identify areas for improvement.

Taking these insights further, conversion rate measures how effectively your site transforms visitors into customers or leads. This metric is vital for understanding the return on investment (ROI) from your SEO efforts. To optimize conversions, consider A/B testing various elements, such as call-to-action buttons and landing page designs, to discover what resonates best with users.

Backlink quality and quantity are also pivotal in assessing SEO performance. Backlinks from authoritative sites signal trustworthiness to search engines and can significantly influence rankings. Monitoring your backlink profile using tools like Moz or Ahrefs enables you to evaluate the strength of your link-building efforts and identify opportunities for acquiring high-quality links.

In today's digital landscape, page load speed has become a critical ranking factor; slow-loading pages can frustrate users and contribute to higher bounce rates. Tools like

Google PageSpeed Insights offer actionable recommendations to enhance load times—optimizing images or reducing server response times can lead to significant improvements.

Click-through rate (CTR) is another important metric that measures how often people click on your link after seeing it in search results. A low CTR suggests that even with good rankings, there may be issues with titles or meta descriptions that fail to entice clicks. Testing different versions can help improve this metric over time.

Engagement metrics such as average session duration and pages per session add further depth to insights about user behavior on your site. Longer session durations typically indicate that users find value in your content; therefore, enhancing content relevance through continuous improvement should remain a priority.

Incorporating user-generated content (UGC) into your metrics tracking offers an innovative approach to measuring engagement and brand loyalty while enriching content quality over time. Encouraging customers to leave reviews or share their experiences online boosts credibility and positively impacts overall SEO performance when these interactions appear across social media channels or review platforms.

Finally, developing custom dashboards tailored to specific KPIs enhances data accessibility and visibility for teams involved in digital marketing initiatives. This facilitates informed decision-making based on real-time data analysis rather than relying solely on periodic reports.

By leveraging these diverse metrics—from organic traffic trends to conversion rates—you empower yourself with actionable intelligence essential for refining strategies aimed at optimizing your online presence in an ever-evolving digital landscape. Understanding these nuances enables professionals not just to react but also to proactively shape their SEO strategies toward greater success as they strive to become industry leaders in their respective niches.

Understanding Google Analytics Data

Exploring Google Analytics unveils a wealth of data that can significantly enhance your SEO strategies. It's not merely about accumulating numbers; it's about transforming these figures into actionable insights. To fully leverage this powerful tool, it's essential to navigate its intricate interface and comprehend the vast array of information it provides.

Starting with the dashboard, you'll find several key areas that give you a snapshot of your website's performance. The "Audience" section offers insights into who is visiting your site, including demographics, interests, and behavior metrics. Understanding these elements can profoundly impact how you tailor your content and marketing efforts. Take this example, if the analytics show a majority of younger visitors, you might want to incorporate trending topics or pop culture references to boost engagement.

Equally important is the "Acquisition" section, which reveals how users are finding your site. This area segments traffic sources—such as organic search, direct visits, and social media referrals—allowing you to identify which SEO campaigns are most effective. If you notice a surge in organic search traffic following a targeted blog post, it could be worthwhile to create more content on similar themes or optimize existing articles to enhance their visibility.

Delving into the "Behavior" section provides further insights into user interactions once they land on your site. The "Site Content" area shows which pages attract the most visitors, while "Landing Pages" focuses on the entry points that capture user interest. For example, if a specific product page receives significant traffic but has a low conversion rate, it presents an opportunity to analyze its content and layout for potential improvements. A/B testing different designs or headlines may reveal what resonates best with your audience.

Beyond basic analytics, Google Analytics offers robust features for tracking goals and conversions. Setting specific goals enables you to monitor actions like form submissions, newsletter signups, or purchases—essentially any interaction that adds value to your site. For an e-commerce platform, tracking the conversion rate from landing page visits to completed sales is crucial for evaluating ROI from your SEO initiatives.

Incorporating event tracking further refines your analysis of user interactions beyond standard page views. You might choose to track clicks on specific links or downloads of resources such as eBooks or whitepapers. This data sheds light on not only what users do but also why they engage with particular elements over others.

Another valuable feature is the "Real-Time" report in Google Analytics. This tool allows you to see how users are interacting with your site at any given moment—who is online, what pages they're viewing, and their traffic sources. Monitoring real-time data can be especially insightful after launching a new campaign or publishing significant content, helping you gauge immediate impacts on traffic and engagement.

Integrating Google Analytics with Google Search Console amplifies the insights you can derive from your data. While Google Analytics focuses on user behavior after their visit, Search Console tracks how your site performs in search results by monitoring impressions and clicks for various keywords and identifying indexing issues. Take this example, if certain keywords generate high impressions but low clicks, it suggests that while users see your listings in search results, they may not find them compelling enough to click through—a potential area for improvement in title tags or meta descriptions.

By analyzing this comprehensive data set, you can gain a clearer understanding of both strengths and weaknesses in your SEO strategy. Pay attention to pages with high exit rates; this may indicate that users aren't finding what they need before leaving.

Tools like Hotjar can help investigate these exit points by revealing user journey pathways that may not align with their expectations.

As we explore metrics reporting within Google Analytics further, custom reports become invaluable for providing tailored insights aligned with your business goals. By designing reports around key performance indicators relevant to your SEO efforts—such as organic traffic growth over time alongside corresponding conversion rates—you streamline data analysis for enhanced strategic planning.

mastering Google Analytics goes beyond merely observing trends; it involves interpreting these trends to make proactive decisions. The interplay between various metrics helps create a comprehensive view that informs ongoing optimization efforts across all aspects of digital marketing—from content creation to link-building initiatives—ensuring that every action taken aligns closely with overarching business objectives.

Effectively leveraging Google Analytics requires continuous assessment of performance metrics and adaptability based on real-world data rather than mere speculation. This cycle of evaluation and adjustment fosters an agile approach to SEO strategy development, positioning businesses for sustained growth in an ever-evolving digital landscape where informed decisions take precedence.

Utilizing Search Console Effectively

Effectively utilizing Google Search Console is crucial for any SEO strategy, serving as a powerful tool to enhance your website's visibility and performance in search results. This platform offers valuable insights into how Google perceives your site, guiding your optimization efforts.

The first step in unlocking the full potential of Google Search Console is verifying ownership of your domain. This essential action grants you access to a wide range of features, including monitoring indexing status and inspecting specific URLs. Once verified, you'll find the dashboard filled with information that lays the groundwork for deeper analysis. The "Performance" report is particularly significant, showcasing key metrics such as clicks, impressions, average position, and click-through rate (CTR) for your site's pages.

Analyzing this data helps you pinpoint which keywords are driving traffic and their effectiveness in terms of visibility. For example, if you notice certain keywords generate high impressions but low CTRs, this indicates an area ripe for improvement. Enhancing title tags or meta descriptions to make them more compelling can encourage users to click through from search results.

Another valuable feature is the "Coverage" report, which details the indexing status of your website's pages. It alerts you to any errors that might prevent search engine crawlers from accessing specific URLs. Addressing these issues—whether they involve 404 errors or server connectivity problems—ensures that all valuable content remains accessible to users. Take this example, if a blog post has unexpectedly dropped from the index due to a 404 error, promptly rectifying this can restore its visibility and bring traffic back.

Exploring the "URL Inspection" tool allows for granular control over individual pages. You can request re-crawling of a URL after making updates or resolving issues. This feature is particularly beneficial when you've implemented changes that could positively influence performance; it signals to Google that your content merits revisiting sooner rather than later.

Additionally, the "Sitemaps" section is often overlooked but plays a vital role in SEO. Submitting an updated sitemap helps Google discover new content quickly and ensures important pages are prioritized for crawling. Regularly updating your sitemap when new posts are published or significant changes occur facilitates a smoother indexing process across your site.

The "Mobile Usability" report also warrants special attention;

with mobile-first indexing becoming standard practice, ensuring an optimal experience on mobile devices is critical. Identifying issues such as closely positioned clickable elements or text that is too small for mobile screens allows you to address these concerns before they impact user experience and rankings.

Also, Google Search Console provides insights into backlinks through the "Links" report, revealing which sites link to yours and the anchor text they use. This information is invaluable for developing strategies to acquire high-quality backlinks or recognizing relationships with authoritative domains that could be further leveraged.

Combining insights from Google Search Console with those from Google Analytics creates a comprehensive overview of both user behavior and site performance. Take this example, if you observe traffic spikes in Analytics corresponding with improved keyword visibility reported in Search Console, it becomes clear that your SEO efforts are yielding results.

Regular engagement with these tools fosters a proactive SEO strategy instead of a reactive one. The insights gathered empower you to make informed decisions regarding content creation, technical enhancements, and marketing strategies— all aimed at improving overall search performance.

As you adapt and refine your approach based on this robust data, remember that consistent monitoring leads to a deeper understanding of trends and patterns over time. By leveraging Google Search Console effectively, you're not merely responding to current metrics; you're anticipating shifts in user behavior and adapting proactively—essential traits for any SEO professional seeking success in an ever-evolving digital landscape.

Tracking Rankings and Visibility

Tracking rankings and visibility is a fundamental element of any successful SEO strategy. To gain a true understanding of how your efforts are yielding results, it's crucial to adopt a systematic approach to monitoring your website's performance in search results. This process starts with selecting the right tools that can provide accurate and meaningful insights.

Begin by identifying the keywords you aim to rank for. This involves conducting keyword research and analyzing user intent. For example, if you operate an e-commerce site specializing in outdoor gear, you might target keywords such as "best hiking boots" or "affordable camping gear." After pinpointing these keywords, utilize tools like Ahrefs or SEMrush to track your rankings over time. These platforms offer detailed reports that illustrate how your site ranks for specific keywords, enabling you to visualize changes and fluctuations effectively.

While monitoring keyword rankings, it's important to look beyond mere position numbers. Focus on metrics like organic traffic and click-through rates (CTR). If you observe an improvement in your ranking for a keyword but see little increase in traffic, investigate potential reasons behind this discrepancy. It may be that competitors have more enticing title tags or meta descriptions, prompting a reevaluation of your on-page SEO elements.

The frequency of tracking these metrics also plays a vital role in your analysis. Although daily checks might be tempting— especially in fast-paced industries—consider adopting a weekly or bi-weekly approach instead. This strategy provides a clearer picture of trends without getting bogged down by short-term fluctuations that may not reflect overarching patterns.

To assess overall visibility, consider utilizing visibility index scores from various SEO tools. This index aggregates data from multiple keywords across your site, offering a more comprehensive view of performance over time. A declining score could indicate the need to reevaluate your content strategy or refine your target keywords.

If applicable to your business model, don't overlook local

rankings. Google My Business insights can reveal how often users discover your business through local searches. Monitoring performance at this granular level is particularly crucial for small businesses seeking to attract local clientele.

Incorporating analytics tools can significantly enhance your understanding of how changes in rankings correlate with user behavior on your site. Take this example, Google Analytics can show you the number of sessions generated from organic search alongside conversion rates. This insight allows you to determine whether visitors find what they need after clicking through from search results.

Custom dashboards can further streamline the tracking process. Platforms like Data Studio enable you to compile various data points—from ranking positions to user demographics—into one visual interface, saving time and presenting information in an actionable format.

It's also beneficial to consider seasonality when tracking metrics. If you're in an industry influenced by seasonal trends —such as retail during the holidays or tax services in spring —adjusting the frequency of your ranking checks during peak times can yield more relevant insights aligned with market behavior.

Lastly, don't underestimate the value of competitor analysis in monitoring visibility and rankings. Understanding where competitors rank for shared keywords can uncover opportunities for improvement and highlight areas where you may need to intensify efforts or pivot strategies entirely.

In summary, effective tracking of rankings and visibility requires more than routine checks; it demands a strategic mindset focused on continuous improvement and adaptation based on real-time data. By leveraging comprehensive analytics tools while keeping an eye on user engagement metrics and shifts in the competitive landscape, you'll be better equipped to monitor and enhance your SEO strategies over time. Each piece of data becomes a stepping stone toward optimizing performance and achieving sustained visibility in an increasingly competitive digital environment.

Conversion Rate Optimization (CRO)

To begin, it's essential to assess your current conversion landscape. Tools like Google Analytics provide valuable data about user behavior on your site. For example, if you notice high bounce rates on certain landing pages, it indicates that visitors aren't finding what they expect. This misalignment might stem from unclear messaging or a subpar user experience. Addressing these issues may involve refining your value propositions or enhancing navigation pathways.

Next, let's highlight the significance of A/B testing—an essential practice in CRO. This method involves creating two versions of a webpage to determine which one performs better in terms of conversions. Take this example, if you run an online clothing store aiming to boost newsletter sign-ups, you could test different calls to action (CTAs), such as "Join our community for exclusive discounts" versus "Subscribe for updates." By directing equal traffic to both versions and analyzing metrics like sign-up rates and engagement levels, you can identify which message resonates more effectively with your audience.

Equally important is the role of copywriting in driving conversions. Compelling copy can evoke emotions and prompt users to take action. Successful campaigns offer valuable inspiration; for example, Dropbox significantly increased their conversions by emphasizing benefits over features in their CTAs during their early growth phase. Crafting persuasive headlines and clearly outlining user benefits can dramatically shape how visitors perceive your offering.

Personalization also plays a critical role in enhancing conversion rates. By leveraging data-driven insights, you can tailor experiences based on user demographics or past behaviors. Imagine an e-commerce site showcasing personalized product recommendations based on previous purchases or browsing history. This customization not only enriches the user experience but also increases the likelihood of conversion as users feel more connected to relevant offerings.

As mobile traffic continues to surge each year, addressing barriers that hinder conversions on mobile devices becomes increasingly important. Ensure your website is optimized for mobile use with fast loading times and intuitive navigation designed for smaller screens. According to research by Google, approximately 53% of mobile users abandon sites that take longer than three seconds to load—an alarming statistic that underscores the need for optimization.

Integrating social proof into your web design can further bolster credibility and encourage conversions. Displaying customer testimonials, reviews, or trust badges indicating secure transactions helps instill confidence in potential buyers who may be hesitant to commit online. Take this example, prominently showcasing reviews from satisfied customers on product pages can significantly influence new customers' purchasing decisions.

Analyzing the entire customer journey provides another layer of insight into improving conversion rates. Tools like heat maps allow you to visualize where users click most frequently on your site or how far down they scroll before losing interest. If heat maps reveal that visitors rarely scroll beyond a certain point on a landing page, it may indicate that crucial information needs to be repositioned higher up or presented differently.

Utilizing exit-intent pop-ups is another effective strategy worth considering—these pop-ups appear when users are about to leave your site without converting. Offering incentives such as discounts or exclusive content can entice users back just before they exit, potentially swaying their decision-making.

Finally, it's vital to continuously iterate based on data and insights gathered from testing efforts and user behavior analysis. CRO is not a one-time initiative; it demands ongoing adjustments informed by analytics and feedback from real users interacting with your site.

By incorporating these strategies into your overall SEO plan, you create a comprehensive framework that not only attracts visitors but also effectively converts them into loyal customers or engaged leads eager for further interaction with your brand. In today's competitive landscape, where consumers expect seamless experiences, mastering conversion rate optimization is essential for transforming clicks into tangible results rather than just numbers on a screen—a key driver for long-term growth and sustainability in this dynamic environment.

Custom Dashboards for Reporting

To begin, it's important to identify the key performance indicators (KPIs) that align with your specific SEO objectives. Commonly tracked metrics include organic traffic, keyword rankings, bounce rates, and conversion rates. However, the selection of KPIs should be tailored to your unique goals. For example, if your focus is on brand awareness, prioritizing impressions and reach is essential. Conversely, if you manage an e-commerce site, tracking conversion rates and revenue generated from organic traffic will be more critical.

After defining your KPIs, the next step is to select the right tools for building your dashboard. Google Data Studio is a popular option due to its ability to integrate seamlessly with various data sources like Google Analytics and Search Console. To get started, connect your data sources in Data Studio by navigating to the "Create" button and selecting "Data Source." This allows you to link Google Analytics or other relevant platforms, enabling real-time updates on your dashboard.

With your data sources connected, it's time to structure your dashboard effectively. Utilize visualizations such as graphs and charts to dynamically represent data; these visuals can quickly convey trends or anomalies at a glance. Take this example, a line graph can illustrate changes in organic traffic over time, while a pie chart can display the distribution of traffic across different channels. Prioritize user experience by ensuring that the dashboard is intuitive and easy to navigate; this way, stakeholders can derive insights without extensive training.

Incorporating filters is another valuable enhancement. Filters allow users to drill down into specific segments of data— for example, tracking organic traffic from different geographic locations. By adding a regional filter, users can analyze performance at a more granular level. This feature enriches analysis and helps identify opportunities tailored to specific audiences.

Regularly reviewing and refining your dashboard based on feedback and evolving business needs is essential. What works today may not remain relevant tomorrow as trends change or new data emerges. Schedule routine audits—monthly or quarterly—to assess whether your KPIs still align with your goals and determine if additional metrics should be added for comprehensive insights.

For those managing multiple websites or client accounts, consider using dashboards that aggregate data across platforms. Tools like SEMrush offer functionalities for managing multiple domains under one umbrella while providing tailored insights for each site. You can customize views for each client or website so that stakeholders only see information pertinent to their interests.

As you incorporate custom dashboards into your workflow, effective communication is vital. Regularly share insights gained from the dashboard with your team or clients—highlight what's working well and where improvements are needed. Providing context around the data fosters collaboration and enhances understanding across teams.

Real-world applications illustrate the power of custom dashboards effectively. Take this example, an e-commerce company utilized a Data Studio dashboard that combined Google Analytics data with sales figures from their platform. They observed a spike in organic traffic that coincided with increased product sales during holiday promotions; this insight prompted them to optimize future campaigns based on those successful strategies.

The true value of custom dashboards lies not only in data visualization but also in their ability to empower teams to make informed decisions swiftly. By presenting essential information clearly and concisely, stakeholders can act quickly on emerging trends or address issues before they escalate.

In summary, creating custom dashboards goes beyond aesthetics; it's about driving actionable insights that lead to improved performance across all facets of SEO. The right setup provides clarity amidst complexity while enabling continuous optimization of strategies tailored to efficiently meet business objectives.

Analyzing User Behavior Patterns

To start, utilize tools like Google Analytics to collect data on user interactions. Metrics such as session duration, page views per session, and bounce rates provide a clear picture of user engagement. Take this example, if you notice visitors spending significantly less time on certain pages, it may indicate that the content isn't meeting their expectations. To gain deeper insights, consider using heatmap tools like Hotjar or Crazy Egg. These tools visualize where users click, scroll, and linger on your site, revealing patterns that standard analytics might overlook and enabling more targeted improvements.

Segmenting your audience is another vital strategy. By categorizing users based on their behaviors—such as first-time visitors versus returning customers—you can tailor content and navigation paths more effectively. For example, returning visitors may appreciate personalized recommendations based on previous interactions, while first-time visitors might require a general introduction to your brand's offerings. This segmentation allows for dynamic adjustments to user experiences, ultimately enhancing engagement and conversion rates.

Once you've gathered quantitative data, complement it with qualitative insights through user feedback. You can achieve this by integrating surveys or feedback forms into your website or sending follow-up emails after purchases. For example, if users consistently mention difficulty finding specific products during checkout, this feedback highlights areas for improvement in navigation or product categorization. Direct input from users ensures that your optimizations align with their actual experiences and needs.

Incorporating A/B testing into your analysis further refines your understanding of user behavior patterns. By creating variations of key pages—such as altering the color of call-to-action buttons or modifying headlines—you can determine which version yields better engagement results. A notable case involved a leading online retailer that tested two different homepage layouts; the version featuring larger images resulted in a 15% increase in conversions over the standard layout. These experiments not only provide actionable insights but also foster a culture of data-driven decision-making within your team.

Another important aspect of user behavior analysis is understanding the customer journey across multiple touchpoints. Users often engage with brands through various channels—such as social media, email newsletters, and organic search—before making a purchasing decision. Mapping out this journey with analytics tools that offer multi-channel attribution modeling helps identify which paths lead to conversions most frequently. Take this example, if social media generates high traffic but low conversions compared to organic search, it may indicate a need for more compelling landing pages or tailored content for social audiences.

Mobile behavior is also critical in today's digital landscape since mobile devices account for a significant portion of web traffic. Analyzing how mobile users navigate your site can reveal specific challenges they face compared to desktop users. If mobile bounce rates are higher than average, this could suggest issues such as slow loading times or non-responsive design elements frustrating mobile visitors. Enhancing mobile usability—through responsive design techniques and optimized page load speeds—ensures a seamless experience across devices.

Finally, implementing tools like Google Tag Manager can streamline the tracking process and facilitate advanced setups without requiring constant code changes on your site. This flexibility allows for real-time adjustments based on observed behavior patterns without needing extensive development resources.

The ultimate aim of analyzing user behavior patterns is not just to gather data but to transform those insights into actionable strategies that resonate with users' needs and preferences. When teams adopt an iterative approach informed by continuous analysis and feedback loops, they position themselves to proactively respond to changing user dynamics while improving their SEO effectiveness.

By deeply understanding user interactions and creatively leveraging those insights within SEO strategies, businesses can cultivate meaningful engagements that lead to higher rankings and improved conversion rates over time.

Automating SEO Reporting

To start, consider the variety of tools available that can streamline your reporting tasks. Google Data Studio stands out as an excellent choice for creating dynamic, customizable dashboards that pull data from multiple sources such as Google Analytics and Google Search Console, as well as third-party platforms like SEMrush or Ahrefs. With Data Studio, you can craft visually appealing reports that automatically update as new data becomes available. For example, you might create a dashboard that showcases organic traffic trends over time, correlating fluctuations with significant events like content launches or marketing campaigns.

Integrating APIs (Application Programming Interfaces) can further enhance the automation of your reporting process. Many SEO tools provide APIs to programmatically extract data. If you're using Ahrefs to monitor backlinks and keyword rankings, for instance, you could write a script to regularly pull this data into a spreadsheet. Utilizing Python along with libraries like Pandas and Requests simplifies this task considerably. A basic script might look like this:

```python
import requests

import pandas as pd


def fetch_data(api_url):

response = requests.get(api_url)

data = response.json()

return pd.DataFrame(data)


api_url = 'https://api.ahrefs.com/v3/site-explorer/metrics?target=yourdomain.com'

data_frame = fetch_data(api_url)

data_frame.to_csv('seo_metrics.csv', index=False)
```

This script allows you to generate CSV files containing the latest SEO metrics automatically, freeing you from manual effort.

In addition to visual dashboards and API integrations, consider utilizing email automation for regular updates. Services like Zapier can connect different applications and send scheduled reports directly to your inbox. For example, you could configure Zapier to send a weekly email summarizing key performance indicators such as organic traffic changes, bounce rates, or conversion metrics from Google Analytics. This setup ensures you receive critical insights without having to log into multiple platforms constantly.

Another valuable strategy is leveraging Google Sheets for real-time collaboration on SEO reports. By linking your Google Sheets with Google Analytics or other data sources through built-in connectors, your team can access live metrics whenever needed. You can incorporate formulas within Sheets to automatically calculate relevant KPIs. Take this example, if you're interested in determining the percentage change in organic traffic month-over-month, you might use:

```plaintext
=(B2 - A2) / A2 * 100
```

Here, B2 represents the current month's traffic while A2 represents the previous month's traffic.

Automation also paves the way for advanced performance tracking solutions. Implementing tools like Google Tag Manager streamlines tagging across your website and enables tracking of custom events without requiring code changes each time new data points need capturing. For example, tracking specific button clicks or form submissions can provide insights into user behavior that inform both content strategy and technical adjustments.

While automation offers powerful advantages, it's crucial not to become complacent about the depth of analysis required. Regularly reviewing automated reports is essential for identifying trends that call for human insight or strategic adjustment. Consider scheduling monthly reviews of your automated reports with your team to discuss findings and refine strategies based on what the data reveals.

Lastly, don't underestimate the importance of defining clear goals regarding what you want from automated reporting. Identify which metrics align best with your business objectives —whether it's improving visibility in search results or enhancing user engagement on site pages—and tailor your automated systems accordingly.

By embracing automation in SEO reporting, professionals position themselves to swiftly adapt to changing conditions while ensuring informed decision-making backed by real-time data insights. This approach not only saves time but also empowers teams to concentrate on driving results through strategic initiatives instead of getting lost in manual data processes. In an ever-evolving digital landscape, those who effectively harness automation will undoubtedly maintain their competitive advantage in the dynamic world of SEO.

CHAPTER 11: SEO FOR E-COMMERCE WEBSITES

Unique Challenges of E-commerce SEO

E -commerce SEO presents a unique set of challenges that require a deep understanding of both search engine optimization principles and the specific characteristics of online retail. Unlike traditional websites, e-commerce platforms often contend with extensive product catalogs, dynamic inventory, and intricate user journeys. These elements create a complex landscape where effective SEO strategies must tackle a variety of technical and content-related issues.

One significant challenge is managing duplicate content, which commonly arises from product variations like size, color, or specifications. When multiple URLs point to similar product pages, search engines may struggle to determine which version should rank higher. To address this issue, implementing canonical tags is essential. Take this example, if you offer two versions of a shirt—one in red and one in blue—each with its own URL, you should designate the preferred version using a canonical tag on the less desirable page. This practice signals to search engines which URL you want indexed while preserving link equity across similar pages.

Another hurdle is optimizing product descriptions for both search engines and users. Many e-commerce sites rely on manufacturer-provided descriptions that often lack uniqueness and detail. To enhance visibility in search results, it's important to create original content that incorporates relevant keywords while also emphasizing the product's features and benefits. Rather than defaulting to a generic description like "high-quality running shoes," consider crafting something more specific: "Experience ultimate comfort with our lightweight running shoes designed for optimal breathability and support during long-distance runs." This approach not only improves SEO but also captivates potential buyers.

Technical elements play an equally vital role in achieving e-commerce SEO success. Site speed is crucial; slow-loading pages can lead to high bounce rates and lost sales opportunities. Utilizing tools like Google PageSpeed Insights can help identify areas for improvement. If image loading times are an issue, techniques such as image compression or using next-gen formats like WebP can significantly enhance load times without compromising quality.

Additionally, structuring your site effectively enhances user experience while bolstering SEO efforts. An intuitive navigation system helps guide users seamlessly from general categories down to specific products. Implementing breadcrumbs allows users to easily trace their path back through categories, reinforcing the website hierarchy for search engines.

Mobile optimization is another critical consideration in today's shopping landscape. A substantial portion of e-commerce traffic now comes from mobile devices, making it imperative for your site to be responsive and easy to navigate on smaller screens. Tools like Google's Mobile-Friendly Test can help assess your site's mobile usability. If issues are detected, adjustments such as larger touch targets for buttons or simplified navigation menus can greatly improve the mobile shopping experience.

Local SEO presents its own challenges for e-commerce businesses aiming to capture hyperlocal advantages. If your e-commerce platform includes physical stores or offers local pickup options, optimizing for local searches becomes essential. Creating location-specific landing pages tailored with local keywords can drive traffic from users searching for nearby services or products available for immediate purchase.

In addition to these technical challenges, building trust is crucial in e-commerce SEO strategies. User reviews not only serve as social proof but also contribute unique content that enhances keyword relevance on product pages. Encouraging customers to leave detailed feedback about their experiences increases authenticity while helping prospective buyers make informed decisions.

Given the ever-evolving nature of algorithms, staying updated on industry changes is critical for maintaining visibility in search results. Monitoring trends through resources like Google's Search Central Blog ensures you remain aware of developments that specifically impact e-commerce practices.

navigating the complexities of e-commerce SEO requires a blend of creativity and analytical thinking. By combining compelling content with solid technical foundations, you can achieve greater online visibility and improved conversion rates. As the landscape continues to evolve rapidly, embracing innovative approaches will be essential for overcoming these unique challenges and maximizing your brand's potential within the competitive realm of online retail.

Product Page Optimization

Product page optimization is a crucial element of e-commerce SEO, significantly impacting both search engine visibility and conversion rates. When users arrive at your product pages, they are often on the verge of making a purchase, seeking more than just information. Therefore, every detail on these pages must be carefully designed to engage visitors and motivate them to take action.

At the heart of effective product page optimization lies the product title. This is not merely a label; it presents an opportunity to incorporate high-value keywords that align with what potential customers are searching for. Instead of using vague titles like "Running Shoes," opt for a more descriptive approach, such as "Men's Lightweight Running Shoes with Breathable Mesh Upper." This specificity not only enhances SEO by catering to user intent but also provides clarity about the product itself.

Following the title, the product description plays a pivotal role in engaging customers. It should do more than reiterate features; it needs to connect with customers' needs and desires. Crafting compelling narratives that emphasize benefits can significantly influence purchasing decisions. Take this example, instead of simply stating "Waterproof jacket," describe it as "Stay dry and comfortable in any weather with our advanced waterproof jacket, featuring breathable fabric technology." This approach appeals to emotions while seamlessly integrating relevant keywords.

High-quality images are essential in the online shopping experience, serving both aesthetic and functional purposes. Showcasing the product from multiple angles helps consumers make informed choices. Including lifestyle images—pictures that demonstrate the product in use—can further enhance emotional appeal. Additionally, optimizing images with descriptive file names and alt text not only aids accessibility but also boosts search engine ranking. For example, instead of naming an image "img_001.jpg," use a format like "mens-lightweight-running-shoes-breathable-mesh.jpg."

Customer reviews are another critical aspect of product page optimization. They enrich your page with valuable content and provide social proof to potential buyers. Encouraging detailed reviews can increase your page's relevance for various queries. Implementing structured data markup can improve how these reviews appear in search results, potentially showcasing star ratings and boosting click-through rates.

Strategic calls-to-action (CTAs) are vital for guiding customers toward making a purchase. While buttons like "Add to Cart" or "Buy Now" may seem straightforward, they play a significant role in influencing user behavior. Experimenting with contrasting colors and placements can enhance engagement rates. A/B testing different CTAs allows you to discover what resonates best with your audience.

In today's mobile-centric world, ensuring mobile optimization is paramount in product page design. As more consumers shop via smartphones and tablets, responsive design that adapts seamlessly to various screen sizes is essential. Mobile users should easily navigate through products, read descriptions, view images, and complete purchases without hassle.

Page load speed is another critical consideration; slow-loading pages can lead to lost sales opportunities. Tools like Google PageSpeed Insights enable you to analyze loading times and identify areas for improvement. Techniques such as compressing images, leveraging browser caching, and minimizing JavaScript can greatly enhance performance.

Additionally, structuring your product pages with clear navigation pathways supports user experience while benefiting SEO by improving crawl efficiency for search engines. Implementing breadcrumbs provides users with visual cues about their location within your site hierarchy and helps search engines understand your page structure better.

Finally, leveraging rich snippets through structured data enhances how your product pages appear in search results beyond standard blue links. By marking up key information such as prices, availability, and ratings using schema.org vocabulary, you increase your chances of standing out in crowded search results.

By focusing on each element of product page optimization—from titles and descriptions to images and CTAs—you create a comprehensive environment that promotes conversions while boosting visibility on search engines. As online retail grows increasingly competitive, mastering these components will ensure that your products not only attract clicks but also convert visits into sales. Embracing creative strategies within these frameworks will be key to distinguishing yourself from competitors in this dynamic marketplace.

Navigational Elements and Site Structure

Navigational elements and site structure are essential for creating an e-commerce website that not only attracts visitors but also drives conversions. A well-organized site enhances the user experience by enabling customers to find what they need quickly and intuitively. When users can navigate your site effortlessly, they are more likely to stay longer and make purchases, ultimately boosting your conversion rates.

The primary navigation menu acts as a roadmap for your site. It should be both concise and comprehensive, offering access to key categories and subcategories that reflect your product offerings. Rather than overwhelming users with too many choices, focus on clarity. A clean layout that logically categorizes products—by type, brand, or use case—helps visitors avoid feeling lost among endless options. For example, if you sell outdoor gear, your main categories could include Camping, Hiking, and Fishing, with each category further divided into relevant subcategories.

Another crucial aspect of navigational design is the use of breadcrumbs. These secondary navigation aids show users their current location within the site hierarchy, making it easier for them to backtrack without hitting the back button repeatedly.

Take this example, a breadcrumb trail like Home > Camping > Tents > Waterproof Tents not only aids navigation but also provides search engines with context about your content structure, enhancing SEO.

Incorporating filters into category pages can significantly improve the user experience. Filters allow customers to narrow down product options based on specific criteria such as size, color, price range, or brand. This feature is especially valuable for large inventories, where browsing through numerous items can become tedious. For example, a shopper searching for running shoes can quickly filter by "Men's," "Size 10," and "Under)100," honing in on their preferences without sifting through every available option.

Search functionality is another vital navigational element that impacts user experience and conversion rates. An effective search bar should return relevant results and support advanced features like autocomplete suggestions and synonyms for common terms. Take this example, if a user types "sneakers," it could suggest related products such as "athletic shoes." Implementing an intelligent search algorithm helps users find products quickly while keeping them engaged with your offerings.

Site structure extends beyond navigation menus; it also involves how product pages interconnect within your website. Each product page should link logically to related items—this can be achieved through cross-selling techniques or curated collections based on customer behavior or seasonal trends. For example, if a customer views a camping tent, suggesting related items like sleeping bags or portable stoves encourages them to explore your offerings further.

Additionally, internal linking plays a crucial role in both SEO performance and usability. By linking relevant content throughout your site—such as blog posts on hiking tips or product guides—you enhance user understanding while helping search engines index your pages more effectively. Each link serves as a pathway leading potential customers deeper into your content ecosystem.

Mobile optimization is another critical consideration when discussing navigational elements and site structure. With the increasing prevalence of mobile shopping, ensuring that menus are responsive is essential. Navigation should adapt seamlessly across devices; consider using collapsible menus on mobile screens to maintain simplicity while maximizing space.

Finally, it's vital that all navigation components load swiftly. Slow-loading elements can lead to frustration and abandoned carts. Regularly test your site's speed using tools like Google PageSpeed Insights and optimize images and other assets accordingly to ensure smooth performance.

A thoughtfully designed navigational system paired with a clear site structure creates an engaging shopping experience that meets customers' needs while enhancing search engine visibility. As you refine these elements of your e-commerce platform, remember: clarity breeds confidence in consumers— the easier you make it for them to find what they want, the more likely they are to complete their purchases without hesitation.

Managing Duplicate Content

Managing duplicate content is a vital aspect of optimizing an e-commerce website. Not only can duplicate content confuse search engines, but it can also dilute the authority of your pages, potentially resulting in lower rankings. This issue often arises from various sources, such as product variations, different URLs for the same product, and user-generated content. By understanding how to effectively manage duplicate content, you can maintain a healthy website and enhance your SEO performance.

The first step is identifying the sources of duplicate content on your site. Product variations are common culprits, especially when the same item is available in different sizes or colors.

For example, if you have a red t-shirt listed alongside a blue one, search engines may struggle to determine which page to prioritize in search results. A practical solution is to implement canonical tags. By specifying a canonical version of a page, you signal to search engines which URL should be treated as the primary source. In this scenario, you would designate one t-shirt page as canonical while treating the others as alternate versions.

Another frequent source of duplication stems from session IDs or tracking parameters added to URLs. These can create multiple URLs leading to the same content, complicating search engines' ability to rank them effectively. To address this issue, consider utilizing URL parameters in your Google Search Console settings or employing robots.txt files to block crawling on these duplicate URLs altogether.

Product descriptions can also contribute to duplicate content issues, particularly when sourced directly from manufacturers or suppliers. If multiple sites feature identical descriptions, Google may hesitate to rank any of those pages highly due to redundancy. To mitigate this issue, focus on crafting unique product descriptions that resonate with your brand voice and target audience. Instead of merely repeating what's found on a manufacturer's website, highlight specifics that matter— consider benefits, features unique to your store, or real-world applications that distinguish your offerings.

User-generated content adds another layer of complexity to managing duplicates. Reviews or comments that echo sentiments expressed elsewhere can trigger duplicate content flags from search engines. One effective tactic is to leverage structured data markup (Schema.org) for reviews and ratings while filtering out duplicate reviews on product pages whenever possible. This approach preserves the originality of user feedback and enriches the snippets displayed in search results.

Regular audits of your site using tools like Screaming Frog

or Sitebulb can further help you manage duplicates effectively. These tools allow you to crawl your site and identify unintended duplication across pages, providing a comprehensive overview for remediation.

Redirects also play an essential role in managing duplicate content. If outdated URLs lead users back to similar products or variants no longer available for sale, implementing 301 redirects can seamlessly guide both users and search engines to updated pages without losing traffic or authority.

Additionally, incorporating XML sitemaps helps combat duplicate content issues by explicitly listing your preferred URLs for search engines. This practice ensures they are aware of which pages are live and relevant, thereby reducing confusion over potential duplicates.

As you implement these strategies for managing duplicate content, remember that clear navigation and organized link structures enhance both user experience and SEO effectiveness. The more streamlined and well-structured your site appears —both in layout and content—the better positioned you'll be within search engine results.

Navigating these challenges requires diligence but yields significant rewards. Enhanced rankings and improved visibility await those who proactively manage their site's integrity against duplications. By incorporating these practices into your daily operations, you can ensure your e-commerce platform thrives amid increasing competition while delivering valuable experiences for users seeking quality products online.

Handling Out-of-Stock Pages

Managing out-of-stock pages is a crucial yet often overlooked component of e-commerce SEO. When products become unavailable, the way you handle these pages can have a significant impact on both your site's visibility and the user experience. Poorly managed out-of-stock pages can confuse customers and hinder search engines from grasping your website's overall relevance.

To address this challenge effectively, start by considering how to enhance the content of these pages rather than simply displaying a generic out-of-stock message. Enrich the page with valuable information, such as estimated restock dates, links to related products that are still available, or suggestions for similar items. This approach not only improves user experience but also helps maintain the page's indexing in search results, preserving its value.

While it may be tempting to redirect out-of-stock pages, proceed with caution. A well-implemented 301 redirect to a similar product can work, but it's essential that the redirected page offers comparable or better options. For example, if a specific model of running shoes is unavailable, redirecting users to another model from the same brand with similar features can be effective. Just make sure that the alternative meets user expectations to avoid disappointment.

In cases where products are permanently discontinued, using a custom 404 page can retain traffic by directing users to relevant sections of your site instead of leaving them stranded. On your 404 page, provide links to best-selling items or popular categories that might capture their interest. Take this example, if a particular gadget is no longer available, you could highlight other electronics that might fulfill similar needs.

Monitoring user behavior on these out-of-stock pages offers valuable insights into customer preferences and trends. Tools like Google Analytics can track interactions—such as whether users click on related items or leave immediately—allowing you to refine your strategy over time.

Implementing structured data markup (Schema.org) on your product pages can further enhance how search engines interpret your inventory status. This markup clarifies whether an item is temporarily out of stock or permanently discontinued, helping search engines better understand how to index and rank these products.

If you manage multiple variations of a product, such as different sizes or colors, it's essential to communicate the availability of each variant clearly. If one size goes out of stock while others remain available, indicate which variants can still be purchased and offer customers the option to sign up for notifications when their preferred size returns.

Email marketing strategies can also play a pivotal role in managing out-of-stock situations effectively. Encourage visitors landing on these pages to subscribe for updates on restocks or similar items through email notifications. This engagement keeps potential buyers connected with your brand during stock shortages and builds loyalty by providing timely information tailored to their interests.

Regularly auditing inventory levels and ensuring accurate information across all channels—such as website listings and social media posts—keeps everything aligned and helps prevent user frustration stemming from misleading availability claims. Implementing an inventory management system that integrates directly with your e-commerce platform can minimize human error and enhance operational efficiency.

how you handle out-of-stock products reflects on your brand's professionalism and reliability in the eyes of both customers and search engines. By employing thoughtful strategies and maintaining clear communication about product availability, you preserve valuable traffic and foster trust, encouraging repeat visits even when certain items are unavailable for purchase.

Navigating stock levels effectively transforms the process from mere reaction to proactive anticipation of customer needs while optimizing for search visibility. Through careful planning and strategic management of out-of-stock situations, you can create opportunities rather than setbacks within your e-commerce strategy.

The Power of User Reviews

Harnessing the power of user reviews can significantly elevate your e-commerce strategy, creating a dynamic environment where customer feedback not only guides potential buyers but also enhances your site's SEO performance. Reviews are more than just testimonials; they represent a rich source of content that both search engines value and users trust.

When prospective customers visit a product page filled with positive reviews, their confidence in the product soars. Take this example, a study by BrightLocal reveals that 79% of consumers trust online reviews as much as personal recommendations. This statistic highlights the importance of actively encouraging customers to share their experiences after making a purchase. By prompting satisfied customers to leave feedback, you create a valuable repository of user-generated content that enhances your product pages with relevant keywords and phrases.

Incorporating these reviews directly onto your product pages not only improves user experience but also boosts search visibility. When displaying reviews, consider emphasizing key elements such as product features, delivery times, and customer service experiences. Utilizing diverse formats—like star ratings and concise text snippets—caters to different browsing preferences. For example, a brief quote such as "Best shoes for running—lightweight and comfy!" accompanied by a star rating can quickly grab attention while conveying essential information.

And, using structured data markup for reviews is an advanced technique that helps search engines better understand this feedback. By implementing Schema.org markup for review data, you clarify the context and relevance of reviews linked to your products. This approach not only aids in indexing but may also result in rich snippets—those visually appealing star ratings displayed directly in search results—which can further enhance click-through rates.

It's equally important to address negative reviews constructively, as they present an opportunity to showcase exceptional customer service. Responding promptly to negative feedback demonstrates to potential buyers that you value their input and are committed to improving your offerings. Take this example, if a review mentions a delayed shipping experience, a thoughtful response acknowledging the issue and proposing a solution can transform a dissatisfied customer into a loyal one. This transparency builds trust—a fundamental pillar of successful e-commerce.

Encouraging user engagement goes beyond merely requesting reviews; it also involves fostering community interaction around your products. Consider integrating platforms where users can ask questions or interact with other buyers about their experiences. A Q&A section on product pages allows potential buyers to gain real-time insights from those who have already made purchases. For example, if someone inquires whether a specific jacket is warm enough for winter, existing customers can share their insights based on their experiences.

Monitoring and analyzing user review sentiment provides valuable insights that can inform product development and marketing strategies. Tools like sentiment analysis software can help sift through vast amounts of feedback to identify trends or common issues with specific products. Take this example, discovering that several customers mention sizing issues could prompt you to revise size descriptions or adjust inventory accordingly.

Incorporating user-generated content into your overall marketing strategy amplifies its impact. Sharing positive reviews across social media channels or in email newsletters not only highlights customer satisfaction but also drives traffic back to product pages. Prominently featuring testimonials on landing pages or advertisements builds credibility and entices new visitors who may be undecided about purchasing.

leveraging user reviews transforms them from simple feedback mechanisms into powerful marketing tools that enhance SEO while fostering community engagement and brand loyalty. The collective voice of satisfied customers creates an authentic narrative around your products that traditional advertising cannot replicate.

Establishing processes for soliciting feedback, openly addressing concerns, analyzing trends within those reviews, and integrating this content into broader marketing initiatives will solidify your brand's reputation while effectively optimizing for search engines. Investing time in managing user reviews not only benefits SEO but also cultivates lasting relationships with customers who feel heard and valued—an invaluable asset in today's competitive e-commerce landscape.

Leveraging Rich Snippets

Rich snippets serve as a powerful asset in the SEO toolkit, enhancing both visibility and engagement within search results. By providing users with additional context about your content before they click through, these enriched listings can significantly influence their decision to visit your site. Effectively leveraging rich snippets can lead to improved click-through rates (CTR) and, ultimately, drive more qualified traffic to your pages.

The first step in utilizing rich snippets is understanding how to implement structured data. This standardized format helps convey information about a webpage and classifies its content. The schema.org vocabulary is commonly used for this purpose, covering various types of content such as articles, products, reviews, and events. Take this example, if you manage an online store, applying structured data to your product listings— marking up details like price, availability, and user ratings—can result in rich snippets that display price ranges or star ratings directly in search results.

To illustrate how to implement structured data, let's consider a recipe website. When marking up a recipe page using JSON-LD (JavaScript Object Notation for Linked Data), you would include essential attributes like the recipe name, cooking time, ingredients, and nutritional information. Here's a simplified example of what that markup might look like:

```json

@context": "https://schema.org",
@type": "Recipe",
name": "Chocolate Chip Cookies",
recipeIngredient": [
2 cups flour",
1 cup sugar",
1 cup chocolate chips
],
cookTime": "PT30M",
nutrition":
@type": "NutritionInformation",
calories": "200 calories


```

After embedding this structured data into your HTML, it's crucial to validate it using tools like Google's Rich Results Test or the Schema Markup Validator. These tools ensure that your markup is implemented correctly and is eligible for rich snippet display in search results.

Monitoring performance after implementation is equally vital. Utilize Google Search Console to track how your rich snippets are performing. Focus on metrics such as impressions and CTR for pages with structured data. If you notice an increase in clicks but low impressions, it may suggest that while users are intrigued by your listing, they aren't seeing it frequently enough —possibly due to keyword targeting issues or competition.

The versatility of rich snippets extends beyond recipes or products; they can enhance various content types, including articles and FAQs. For example, if you maintain a blog post addressing frequently asked questions on a specific topic, implementing FAQ schema can yield rich snippets featuring those questions and answers directly in search engine results pages (SERPs). This approach not only boosts visibility but also establishes your authority on the subject matter.

Consider a local business aiming to attract more customers via search engines. By incorporating local business schema markup on their homepage—outlining key details such as address, phone number, operating hours, and service area—they can significantly improve their search presence. This information will appear in searches relevant to their services and location, making them more appealing to potential customers seeking immediate assistance nearby.

Staying informed about the evolution of different types of rich snippets is also essential, as search engines continuously refine their algorithms and presentation formats. Engaging with SEO communities or following industry news can provide valuable insights into emerging trends in structured data usage.

Integrating rich snippets into your overall SEO strategy goes beyond merely adding code; it enhances user experience and increases engagement from the moment potential visitors see your site listed in search results. By effectively presenting your content with structured data and rich snippets, you boost the likelihood of user interaction—which translates into greater traffic and potentially higher conversion rates.

rich snippets elevate your digital presence by transforming standard listings into eye-catching entries that convey crucial information upfront. As you incorporate these strategies into your workflow, remember that the goal is not only visibility but also building trust—creating an inviting first impression that encourages users to explore further while establishing credibility within your niche.

Technical SEO for E-commerce

Technical SEO for e-commerce is a complex but essential aspect of managing an online store. It not only helps attract traffic but also plays a vital role in converting visitors into customers. Unlike traditional websites, e-commerce platforms face unique challenges and opportunities regarding search engine visibility. A thoughtfully optimized site architecture, combined with a robust technical foundation, can propel an e-commerce website from obscurity to prominence in search results.

At the heart of technical SEO is the site's architecture. An intuitive and logical structure allows both users and search engines to navigate your offerings with ease. Start by organizing your products into clear categories and subcategories. Take this example, if you sell clothing, your structure might look like this:

- Home
- Men's Clothing
- Shirts
- Pants
- Accessories
- Women's Clothing
- Dresses
- Tops
- Shoes

This hierarchical organization enhances user experience while enabling search engines to crawl and index your pages more efficiently. Incorporating breadcrumbs can further improve navigation by allowing users to easily trace their steps back to higher-level pages.

Next, focus on optimizing product pages. Each product should have its own dedicated page featuring unique content that highlights its features and benefits. Avoid duplicating content across listings; instead, create rich descriptions that naturally incorporate targeted keywords. For example, when selling a pair of running shoes, emphasize specific features like comfort technology or material benefits in a way that resonates with potential buyers while appealing to search engine algorithms.

Image optimization is another crucial aspect of e-commerce SEO. High-quality images are vital for effectively showcasing products, but they can slow down loading times if not managed properly. Use formats like WebP for superior compression without compromising quality, and ensure each image has descriptive alt text. This approach not only enhances accessibility but also provides search engines with additional context about your visual content.

Page speed significantly influences user experience and SEO performance. Utilize tools like Google PageSpeed Insights to assess your site's loading times and identify areas for improvement. Common optimizations include minimizing HTTP requests, leveraging browser caching, and using Content Delivery Networks (CDNs) to deliver content more efficiently across different regions.

In today's marketplace, mobile optimization is essential as mobile shopping continues to grow rapidly. Ensure your e-commerce site is fully responsive, seamlessly adapting across devices, and incorporates touch-friendly elements for easy navigation on smartphones and tablets. With Google's mobile-first indexing, the mobile version of your website will primarily be used for ranking purposes; thus, it must provide an experience as robust as its desktop counterpart.

Secure transactions are critical in e-commerce; a secure site fosters trust with customers and positively impacts your rankings. Acquire an SSL certificate to enable HTTPS, encrypting user data during transactions. This not only safeguards customer information but also enhances SEO rankings since Google considers site security in its algorithmic evaluations.

Structured data is vital for boosting the visibility of product listings through rich snippets—information such as price, availability, and review ratings can be marked up using schema.org vocabulary. For example:

```json

@context": "https://schema.org",

@type": "Product",

name": "Running Shoes",

image": "https://example.com/images/running-shoes.jpg",

description": "Comfortable running shoes with advanced cushioning technology.",

brand":

@type": "Brand",

name": "FitRun

,

sku": "FR12345",

offers":

@type": "Offer",

url": "https://example.com/running-shoes",

priceCurrency": "USD",

price": "79.99",

itemCondition": "https://schema.org/NewCondition",
```

availability": "https://schema.org/InStock

` ` `

Implementing structured data can enhance click-through rates by providing potential buyers with valuable information directly within search results.

Lastly, regular monitoring and auditing of technical aspects are essential for maintaining optimal performance over time. Tools like Screaming Frog or Ahrefs can help identify crawl errors or broken links that could detract from user experience and harm your rankings if left unaddressed.

In summary, mastering technical SEO for e-commerce requires a comprehensive approach that focuses on site architecture, product page optimization, image handling, speed enhancements, mobile responsiveness, secure transactions, structured data implementation, and ongoing monitoring. By diligently addressing these areas, you establish a strong foundation for improved visibility and increased sales conversion rates—ultimately setting the stage for greater success in the competitive e-commerce landscape.

Order and Shipping Optimization

Order and shipping optimization is essential for the success of any e-commerce business. In today's market, customers have high expectations for delivery speed, accuracy, and transparency. By refining these processes, businesses can not only boost customer satisfaction but also enhance operational efficiency, ultimately leading to increased sales and repeat purchases.

To begin with, it's vital to streamline your order processing system. A well-organized order management system (OMS) should integrate seamlessly with your e-commerce platform. This integration ensures that every order is captured accurately and processed promptly. Take this example, utilizing platforms like Shopify or WooCommerce can automate inventory management and provide real-time updates to customers about their order status. Automation not only reduces the likelihood of human error but also minimizes delays in processing.

Next, enhancing your shipping options is crucial. Offering multiple shipping methods allows you to cater to diverse customer preferences. Some may choose standard shipping for cost savings, while others might opt for expedited options for quicker delivery. By partnering with various carriers, you can compare rates and delivery times, presenting the best choices to customers at checkout.

In addition, implementing a shipping calculator on your website can greatly improve the customer experience. This tool gives customers an estimate of shipping costs based on their location and chosen method before they complete their purchase. By providing this transparency, you help set clear expectations, which can reduce cart abandonment rates.

Packaging is another important aspect of optimization. Invest in materials that protect your products while minimizing weight to lower shipping costs. Thoughtful packaging not only enhances the unboxing experience but also reinforces your brand image. Incorporating branded elements like custom tape or tissue paper adds a personal touch that delights customers and encourages them to share their experiences on social media.

Data analytics also plays a crucial role in optimizing orders and shipping. Utilize analytics tools to track key performance indicators (KPIs), such as average order fulfillment time, shipping costs per order, and customer feedback regarding delivery experiences. Platforms like Google Analytics or specialized logistics software offer valuable insights that can inform your decision-making processes.

And, a robust returns management system should be part of your optimization strategy. A streamlined returns process fosters customer trust and loyalty. Make sure your return policies are clearly communicated on your website so customers easily understand how to return items if necessary. Providing pre-paid return labels can simplify the process, reducing friction for the customer.

Additionally, leveraging technology enhances order tracking capabilities significantly. Implement systems that allow customers to track their orders in real-time through notifications or a dedicated tracking page on your site. Maintaining transparency throughout the shipping process builds trust and alleviates anxiety about when their orders will arrive.

Finally, establishing strong relationships with your suppliers and logistics partners is key. Regular communication helps ensure that inventory levels are sufficient for fulfilling orders promptly while minimizing backorders or stockouts that can frustrate customers. Collaborative planning often leads to more efficient operations and faster deliveries.

By adopting a comprehensive approach to order and shipping optimization—focusing on seamless technology integration, offering diverse shipping options, enhancing packaging experiences, utilizing data analytics effectively, managing returns efficiently, and fostering strong partnerships—you can create a streamlined process that not only meets but exceeds customer expectations. This commitment to excellence distinguishes your e-commerce business in a competitive marketplace and drives long-term growth and success.

CHAPTER 12: FUTURE TRENDS AND INNOVATIONS IN SEO

The Role of Blockchain in SEO

Blockchain technology is gaining recognition for its transformative potential across various industries, including search engine optimization (SEO). Its decentralized nature presents unique advantages that can fundamentally reshape our approach to data integrity, transparency, and user trust in SEO practices. In a time when data breaches and misinformation are prevalent, the robust security features of blockchain can help create a more reliable digital environment.

One of the most compelling aspects of blockchain is its ability to maintain transparent records of information. Each transaction or change made on a blockchain is recorded in a public ledger that is immutable and verifiable by all participants. This transparency can be particularly beneficial for SEO, especially in areas like link building. Since link acquisition strategies often depend heavily on trust—such as guest blogging or influencer partnerships—blockchain can serve as a tool to authenticate these links. For example, if a website can demonstrate via blockchain that it has secured links from reputable sources, it may enhance its authority in the eyes of search engines.

To illustrate this, consider a brand working with various bloggers to promote a product. Traditional methods can make it difficult to ensure that backlinks originate from credible sites and are not part of deceptive link schemes. By implementing blockchain technology, all parties involved could track these links back to their sources. This level of verification may lead search engines to prioritize sites that openly share their link-building history on a blockchain platform.

The emergence of decentralized search engines further highlights how blockchain can disrupt conventional SEO practices. These platforms emphasize user privacy and data ownership, standing in stark contrast to traditional search engines that often monetize user data without offering compensation. As privacy concerns grow among users, decentralized search engines leveraging blockchain could see increased adoption. This shift will require businesses to rethink their SEO strategies to optimize for these emerging platforms.

Additionally, smart contracts—self-executing agreements with terms written directly into code—can streamline processes within SEO campaigns. Imagine automating payments to content creators based on performance metrics established in advance through smart contracts. This automation minimizes disputes over compensation and ensures that creators are fairly rewarded for their contributions based on agreed-upon success indicators such as engagement rates or click-through rates.

The implications of blockchain extend beyond content creation and link building; they also influence how businesses manage their own data. A blockchain-based system allows companies to maintain control over their information while selectively sharing necessary data with search engines or partners. This supports an environment where accuracy is paramount, reducing the likelihood of errors from outdated or incorrect information impacting rankings.

Data ownership enhances user experience as well. When users feel assured that their information is securely stored and shared only when necessary, they are likely to engage more willingly with brands online. For SEO professionals, this underscores the importance of trust-building measures in their strategies. Creating high-quality content becomes even more crucial as users increasingly seek reliable sources over those perceived as dubious.

And, blockchain's ability to provide real-time data can revolutionize keyword research and analytics approaches in marketing campaigns. Traditional analytics tools often have lag times in reporting that can hinder timely decision-making. In contrast, real-time insights generated through blockchain networks empower SEO specialists to adjust their strategies swiftly based on current user behavior trends.

As organizations begin exploring these technologies, it's vital to stay ahead by understanding how blockchain will influence not only technical aspects but also user interactions with brands online. Preparing for this future requires an agile mindset among SEO professionals who recognize potential shifts in user behavior driven by new technologies.

Embracing blockchain technology opens up exciting possibilities for enhancing SEO practices while fostering transparency and trust between users and brands. By integrating these advanced solutions into your strategy now, you position yourself at the forefront of an evolving landscape where digital marketing transcends traditional boundaries, paving the way for innovative approaches in optimizing search visibility well into the future.

Continued Rise of Voice and Visual Search

The rapid adoption of voice and visual search technologies is largely fueled by advancements in artificial intelligence and changing consumer behaviors. As people increasingly prioritize convenience and speed in their digital interactions, optimizing for these search modalities has become essential for SEO professionals. Voice search, once considered a novelty, is now a mainstream feature of daily life, thanks to the widespread use of smart speakers and voice assistants.

This shift towards voice search significantly impacts keyword strategy. Traditional SEO has primarily focused on text-based queries—typically short phrases or keywords. However, voice searches tend to be more conversational and longer. For example, someone might type "best coffee shop," but a voice query could be phrased as, "What's the best coffee shop near me that's open right now?" This evolution calls for a reevaluation of keyword research techniques. To adapt, SEO experts should emphasize natural language processing and consider the types of questions users are likely to ask aloud. Tools like AnswerThePublic can help identify common queries related to a topic, enabling marketers to create content that directly addresses these specific questions.

In addition to voice search, visual search is another transformative trend reshaping user behavior. Consumers can now take pictures of objects and receive instant information about them through platforms like Google Lens. This change in how users interact with search engines necessitates that brands optimize their images effectively. Utilizing high-quality images with descriptive filenames and alt text is crucial for helping search engines understand and index visual content. Take this example, retailers should ensure that product images are tagged with relevant keywords reflecting what users might be searching for visually.

Context plays a vital role in the effectiveness of these emerging search technologies. Since voice and visual searches are often tied to immediate needs or specific situations, businesses must provide clear answers in structured formats. Featured snippets or position zero entries become increasingly important as they cater directly to voice queries. Implementing schema markup can significantly enhance visibility in these areas by helping search engines comprehend the context of the information presented.

And, understanding user intent behind voice and visual searches is crucial for effective optimization. Recognizing the different contexts in which these searches occur—such as urgent needs versus exploratory inquiries—enables marketers to tailor their content more precisely. For example, a consumer visually searching for "blue running shoes" may be looking to make an immediate purchase rather than simply browsing options. Crafting landing pages that focus on conversion tactics for these types of searches can have a direct impact on sales outcomes.

A noteworthy example of successful adaptation is retail giant Target. By integrating visual search technology into its mobile app, Target allows customers to upload photos of products they like while providing instant purchasing options or suggestions for similar items available online or in-store. This seamless integration enhances the shopping experience and increases conversion rates, as consumers can quickly find what they want without the friction typically associated with traditional searching methods.

As reliance on voice-activated devices grows in both homes and public spaces, brands must also optimize their local SEO strategies for voice searches. Many users conduct local searches using voice queries; thus, ensuring accurate information on Google My Business listings is essential. Including relevant details such as business hours, location specifics, and customer reviews improves visibility when users ask their devices for nearby recommendations.

While embracing these trends presents incredible opportunities for visibility and engagement, it also demands constant vigilance to keep pace with evolving algorithms that dictate how search engines interpret and rank voice and visual content. Staying informed about updates from major players like Google can help SEO professionals anticipate changes in ranking factors relevant to these technologies.

As consumers continue gravitating toward instant answers delivered through voice and visual interfaces, integrating these strategies will not only enhance visibility but also deepen user engagement by meeting their immediate informational needs. This forward-thinking approach positions businesses favorably within a competitive landscape as they harness the power of emerging technologies that are redefining search optimization today.

The Impact of Augmented Reality on Search

Augmented Reality (AR) has transitioned from a futuristic concept to a vital component of the digital marketing landscape, fundamentally changing how consumers engage with brands and products. As AR technology continues to evolve, its influence on search and SEO strategies becomes increasingly evident. Today's users are not merely searching for information; they are looking for immersive experiences that enhance their decision-making processes.

Take, for example, the way AR can revolutionize product visualization. Imagine a consumer shopping for furniture online. With AR, they can utilize their smartphones to see how a specific couch would look in their living room before making a purchase. This capability not only affects buying decisions but also transforms retailers' approaches to SEO. Brands must now optimize their content for these interactive experiences, making high-quality images, 3D models, and detailed descriptions essential assets.

This shift also has significant implications for keyword strategies. Traditional text-based searches are evolving into queries that prioritize specific interactive content. Take this example, instead of simply searching for "buy shoes online," a user might ask, "show me how these shoes look on my feet." This evolution underscores the need for natural language processing in keyword research, emphasizing conversational phrases that align with users' intentions for immersive experiences.

To fully leverage AR's potential in search, companies should implement schema markup designed for augmented experiences. This markup signals to search engines that a product is compatible with AR, enabling richer search results that showcase the interactive elements available to users. By incorporating AR-specific tags in product listings, retailers can enhance their chances of appearing in search results when consumers seek items that offer augmented reality features.

A compelling example of this is IKEA's mobile app, which allows users to visualize furniture within their own spaces using AR technology. This app significantly boosts user engagement by enabling interaction with products before purchase. By adopting such innovative solutions, IKEA has not only improved customer satisfaction but also optimized its online presence for relevant AR-related searches.

And, as brands embrace AR strategies, the importance of local SEO becomes paramount. Many users will engage with AR content while exploring their surroundings—think tourists searching for nearby attractions or locals looking for dining options. Ensuring accurate business information across platforms like Google My Business will enhance visibility when users seek local experiences enriched by augmented reality.

However, integrating AR into SEO does present challenges. Maintaining a high-quality user experience requires considerable investment in technology and ongoing updates to keep pace with changing consumer expectations. Additionally, businesses must ensure compatibility across various devices and platforms to avoid alienating potential customers who may not have access to the latest technology.

As we navigate this transformative landscape, understanding

user intent becomes increasingly critical. What motivates users to engage with AR? Are they looking for information or immediate solutions? Recognizing these nuances enables marketers to create targeted content that resonates with consumers at different stages of their buying journey.

The future trajectory of augmented reality in search indicates that consumers will increasingly expect seamless interactions between the digital and physical worlds. Brands that invest in developing compelling AR experiences are likely to capture greater market share by meeting these evolving expectations head-on.

embracing augmented reality as part of your SEO strategy signifies a commitment to innovation and customer-centricity. As search behaviors shift toward more interactive formats, positioning your brand as a leader in this space will not only enhance visibility but also cultivate deeper connections with your audience—transforming casual browsers into engaged customers eager to explore what your brand offers through the lens of augmented reality.

Influencer SEO and Its Role

Influencer SEO is quickly becoming a fundamental aspect of modern digital marketing, merging traditional SEO tactics with the personal touch that social media influencers offer. Unlike conventional methods that primarily focus on keyword optimization and backlinks, influencer SEO utilizes the credibility and extensive reach of individuals who have built loyal followings. This evolution signifies a significant shift in how brands engage with their audiences, positioning influencer partnerships as a crucial strategy for enhancing search visibility.

One of the unique advantages influencers provide to SEO is their ability to create authentic content that resonates deeply with their followers, fostering trust and engagement. For example, when an influencer discusses sustainable fashion in a blog post, their audience is far more likely to visit the brand's website than if the same message were delivered through a generic advertisement. This authenticity not only generates higher engagement—measured through likes, shares, and comments—but also positively impacts search rankings. As search engines increasingly prioritize content that encourages genuine interaction, influencer-generated content becomes exceptionally valuable.

To effectively weave influencer SEO into your overall marketing strategy, begin by identifying influencers whose values align with your brand's mission. Tools like BuzzSumo or Followerwonk can assist in finding suitable candidates by evaluating their reach and engagement metrics. Once you have established partnerships, collaboration is vital. Encourage influencers to produce high-quality content that seamlessly integrates relevant keywords and includes links to your site. Take this example, if a beauty influencer reviews your skincare line, they should naturally incorporate specific keywords that potential customers might be searching for—such as "best anti-aging cream" or "natural skincare routine.

The mechanics of this approach extend beyond simple mentions; when influencers create content centered around your brand, it's crucial they utilize optimized titles and descriptions that follow SEO best practices. Doing so not only enhances the chances of appearing in search results but also enriches the user experience by delivering valuable information. An effective title could be "Top 5 Natural Skincare Products Recommended by Experts," which appeals to both search engines and users alike.

Monitoring the impact of your influencer campaigns on SEO metrics is essential to assess their effectiveness. Utilizing tools like Google Analytics can help you track referral traffic from influencer links and evaluate engagement levels on your site after promotions. If you notice a surge in traffic following a specific influencer's campaign, it indicates a successful partnership worth maintaining or expanding.

Local SEO also plays an integral role in influencer marketing. When influencers with local followings promote nearby businesses or services, they can drive significant traffic to those establishments' websites. For example, if a food blogger highlights a new restaurant opening in town, this not only boosts exposure but also positions the restaurant favorably within local search results as it gains traction through social media engagement.

However, navigating the landscape of influencer SEO does present challenges. Brands must maintain transparency regarding sponsored content to uphold trust and comply with regulations established by agencies like the Federal Trade Commission (FTC). Clear disclosures are essential for fostering honesty between brands and audiences while reducing the risk of backlash against perceived dishonesty.

As you explore this strategy further, keep an eye on emerging platforms where influencers thrive. TikTok has rapidly risen as a key player for engaging younger audiences; brands that effectively tap into its viral nature can achieve remarkable visibility when collaborating with influencers who excel at creating compelling short-form content.

remember that influencer SEO transcends mere collaboration; it's about nurturing long-term relationships with influencers who genuinely resonate with your brand's mission and values. Establishing ongoing partnerships can lead to sustained authenticity in messaging and deeper connections with audiences over time.

At its core, embracing influencer SEO involves leveraging the power of personal branding within today's digital landscape. As consumers increasingly seek personalized experiences online, harnessing influencers' reach can elevate your brand's visibility while cultivating authentic connections that drive both traffic and conversion rates. Adopting this strategy positions you not only as a participant in the evolving SEO arena but also as an innovative leader ready to adapt to shifting consumer expectations.

Mobile-First Indexing and Beyond

Mobile-first indexing marks a significant evolution in how search engines assess and rank websites. Traditionally, search engines focused on indexing desktop versions of sites, but as mobile usage skyrocketed, this method became increasingly inadequate. Today, Google and other major search engines primarily rely on the mobile version of a site for indexing and ranking. This shift emphasizes the necessity for businesses to prioritize mobile optimization in their SEO strategies.

The rise of mobile-first indexing closely aligns with changing user behaviors. Recent studies show that over half of all web traffic now originates from mobile devices, highlighting a clear preference for accessing information on-the-go rather than being confined to desktop computers. That's why, if your website isn't optimized for mobile users, you risk losing valuable traffic and potential conversions. With Google's transition to mobile-first indexing, your site's performance on mobile devices directly affects its visibility in search results.

To navigate this new landscape effectively, start by ensuring your website employs responsive design techniques. Responsive design allows your site to adapt seamlessly to various screen sizes, delivering an optimal viewing experience across devices. This approach not only enhances usability but also improves loading speeds—crucial for retaining visitors. Take this example, a slow-loading page can quickly drive away users on their smartphones, negatively impacting bounce rates.

Content accessibility is another critical element of mobile optimization. Information should be presented in a concise and easily navigable manner on mobile devices. Consider using larger fonts and ensuring buttons are adequately spaced for touch interaction. Features like collapsible menus or accordions can keep content organized without overwhelming users at first glance. For e-commerce sites, simplifying the checkout process on mobile can significantly lower cart abandonment rates.

Images also demand careful attention within a mobile-first strategy. High-resolution images can slow down page loading times on mobile networks, so optimizing them for quicker delivery without sacrificing quality is essential. Tools like TinyPNG can effectively compress images while maintaining visual integrity. Additionally, adopting modern formats like WebP can further enhance load speeds and improve image quality across devices.

Utilizing tools such as Google's Mobile-Friendly Test or PageSpeed Insights can provide valuable insights into your website's performance. These tools analyze loading speed, usability, and overall functionality on various devices, offering actionable recommendations to enhance the mobile experience.

User engagement metrics are also vital for assessing your site's performance under the mobile-first indexing model. Pay close attention to click-through rates (CTR) and average session duration for mobile users compared to those on desktop. Significant disparities—such as lower CTRs or shorter sessions —may indicate areas that require improvement.

Structured data is another important factor that helps search engines understand your content across different devices. Implementing schema markup can provide search engines with additional context about your offerings, increasing the likelihood of appearing in rich snippets or featured results— both of which are particularly advantageous on smaller screens.

Beyond merely adapting existing content for mobile users, consider creating unique experiences tailored specifically for them. Mobile apps can enhance your web presence by offering features like push notifications or location-based services that significantly boost user engagement—elements that traditional websites may struggle to replicate.

As voice search continues to gain popularity among smartphone users, optimizing for voice queries is becoming increasingly important within mobile SEO strategies. Incorporating conversational keywords and phrases that reflect natural language patterns will align better with how people verbally communicate with their devices.

In summary, embracing a mobile-first approach goes beyond compliance with current indexing practices; it is a crucial strategy for enhancing user experience and boosting online visibility. The shift toward prioritizing mobile optimization reflects broader changes in consumer behavior, favoring immediate access to information and services.

By integrating this understanding into your SEO framework, you position yourself ahead of competitors who may still rely heavily on outdated desktop-centric strategies. As technology continues to evolve—especially with advancements like 5G connectivity—the opportunities afforded by superior mobile experiences will only expand further in the digital marketing landscape.

The Growing Importance of UX

The growing importance of user experience (UX) in SEO is increasingly recognized. As search engines evolve, they prioritize user satisfaction as a critical factor in their ranking algorithms. Google's commitment to delivering the best possible experience for users has fundamentally changed how websites are evaluated and ranked. That's why, SEO strategies must now embed UX principles at their core, moving beyond simple keyword optimization to encompass a comprehensive understanding of visitor interactions with content.

Imagine a user landing on your website; their first impressions are formed within seconds. Elements such as page load speed, mobile responsiveness, and intuitive navigation play significant roles in determining whether they stay or return to search results. Take this example, research by Google reveals that

53% of mobile users abandon sites that take longer than three seconds to load. This striking statistic highlights the urgency of optimizing site speed—strategies like compressing images, utilizing browser caching, and minimizing server response times can dramatically enhance load times and keep users engaged.

Equally important is the structure of your website. A well-organized site architecture guides users effortlessly through content, creating clear pathways that encourage engagement. Features like breadcrumbs can significantly enhance navigational clarity, providing users with a sense of direction while also improving internal linking structures that help search engines understand content hierarchy.

Content itself is another crucial element in enhancing UX. It should be easily scannable, employing headers, bullet points, and visuals to break up text and facilitate quick comprehension. For example, when crafting an article about healthy eating tips, using lists or infographics can communicate information more effectively than dense paragraphs alone. Additionally, incorporating multimedia elements such as videos or podcasts caters to various learning preferences and encourages users to spend more time on your page.

Understanding the emotional journey of your audience is vital in this context. Positive experiences lead to higher engagement rates, signaling to search engines that your site holds value. Techniques like A/B testing can help identify what resonates with your audience—be it different layouts or calls-to-action. Analyzing user behavior through tools like heatmaps provides insights into where users click most frequently and where they lose interest, informing necessary adjustments.

Mobile optimization is another critical factor that cannot be overlooked. With mobile-first indexing becoming standard across search engines, ensuring that your site is responsive is essential. This involves not just a mobile-friendly design but also consideration of touch interactions and visual hierarchies tailored for smaller screens.

Also, accessibility enhancements can significantly improve UX for all users, including those with disabilities. Implementing alt text for images and ensuring color contrast meets guidelines fosters a more inclusive web experience. This approach broadens your audience and can also boost search rankings, as search engines increasingly favor sites that accommodate diverse user needs.

As businesses come to recognize the intrinsic connection between UX and SEO performance, many are integrating UX teams into their digital marketing strategies. Companies like Airbnb exemplify this trend; by prioritizing user experience, they have seen improved customer loyalty and organic traffic growth. Their focus on creating an enjoyable booking process and an aesthetically pleasing interface has cultivated trust among users—an essential factor that translates into higher conversion rates.

In light of these insights, excelling in SEO today necessitates a user-centric mindset. This approach not only enhances rankings but also fosters lasting relationships with visitors who are more likely to return and convert if they feel valued throughout their journey on your site. Thus, investing in UX becomes not just an option but a necessity for those aiming to succeed in the competitive landscape of online visibility.

as we explore the relationship between SEO and UX throughout this guide, it becomes clear that prioritizing user experience aligns seamlessly with the evolving demands of search engines. The synergy between effective content delivery and exceptional usability will form the backbone of successful digital strategies moving forward—one where both visitors and algorithms thrive together in harmony.

Privacy and Data Security

The growing emphasis on privacy concerns and data security

is significantly transforming the landscape of SEO and digital marketing. As consumers become more aware of their online privacy, organizations must adjust their strategies to prioritize transparency and trust. This evolution stems not only from consumer demand but also from increasingly stringent regulations designed to protect personal information.

The implementation of GDPR in Europe, along with similar regulations worldwide, has compelled businesses to rethink their approaches to data collection, management, and usage. Companies are now required to explicitly obtain user consent for data collection and provide clear explanations regarding its intended use. Noncompliance can lead to substantial fines and reputational damage, making it essential for SEO professionals to understand these legal frameworks as they develop sustainable strategies that respect user privacy while still achieving marketing objectives.

Search engines, particularly Google, are integrating privacy considerations into their ranking algorithms. For example, the introduction of the "Privacy Sandbox" reflects this trend, aiming to strike a balance between user privacy and advertisers' needs by exploring new methods of targeting users without relying on third-party cookies. That's why, SEO strategies must now pivot towards first-party data collection methods—such as gathering information directly from users through newsletters, membership sign-ups, or loyalty programs.

Data security goes beyond mere compliance; it has a direct impact on user experience and trust. Websites perceived as secure encourage greater user engagement. By implementing HTTPS, encrypting user data, and adopting robust security measures, businesses can enhance their credibility with both users and search engines. Research says that sites utilizing HTTPS tend to rank higher in search results due to the secure connections they provide, reaffirming Google's commitment to promoting safe browsing practices.

The significance of clear privacy policies cannot be overstated. An accessible, easy-to-understand privacy policy reassures users about how their information will be utilized. Detailing data retention periods, third-party sharing practices, and opt-out mechanisms fosters transparency. By prominently linking this information—perhaps in the footer of your website—you not only increase user trust but also comply with regulatory demands.

Gathering user feedback on privacy practices can further refine your approach. Surveys and feedback tools can gauge user sentiment regarding your data handling practices, enabling you to adjust policies that align with audience expectations and enhance customer relations.

Building a reputation for respect towards user data is essential; companies like Apple exemplify this strategy by positioning themselves as advocates for privacy, thereby cultivating strong brand loyalty. Their marketing efforts explicitly communicate a commitment to user protection, resonating with consumers and significantly elevating trust levels.

And, as algorithm updates increasingly factor site safety into ranking criteria, it is crucial for SEO professionals to proactively address potential vulnerabilities. Regular security audits can identify weaknesses before they escalate into serious issues. Utilizing tools like security scanners or employing web application firewalls (WAF) ensures vulnerabilities are promptly addressed, maintaining both security integrity and SEO performance.

adopting a comprehensive perspective on privacy and data security aligns your SEO strategy with consumer values while enhancing your site's authority in the eyes of search engines. This shift towards privacy-centric strategies represents a broader movement—where ethical considerations are woven into business objectives—creating opportunities for innovative approaches in digital marketing.

By embracing these principles, organizations not only protect themselves from legal repercussions but also foster an environment where users feel secure engaging with content. This combination of trustworthiness and operational integrity is likely to result in organic traffic growth and improved conversion rates over time. As businesses commit to integrating robust data protection measures into their core strategies, they lay the groundwork for resilient relationships with their audiences—an essential factor for long-term success in today's rapidly evolving digital marketplace.

Preparing for the Next Major Algorithm Update

Anticipating significant algorithm updates is crucial for maintaining a competitive edge in SEO. The unpredictable nature of search engine algorithms means that proactive preparation can be the key to seizing opportunities rather than falling behind. By engaging with the latest trends and analyzing how past updates have transformed the search landscape, SEO professionals can better adapt to future changes.

Historically, major algorithm updates have focused on enhancing user experience and refining content interpretation. For example, Google's Panda update targeted high-quality content while penalizing sites with thin or duplicate material. Similarly, the Penguin update aimed at eliminating manipulative link-building practices. These trends indicate that upcoming updates will likely continue to emphasize user-centric factors—such as content relevance, authority, and overall user satisfaction—over simplistic SEO tactics.

To effectively prepare for these changes, cultivating a habit of continuous learning is essential. Following industry news from trusted sources like Search Engine Journal or Moz keeps you informed of the latest developments. Engaging with communities on platforms such as Reddit or LinkedIn can provide real-time insights into evolving best practices, while subscribing to newsletters from SEO thought leaders offers unique perspectives that inform strategic pivots.

Conducting regular audits of your current SEO practices is also vital in identifying vulnerabilities and areas for improvement. Begin by evaluating your website's content quality, technical performance, and backlink profile. Tools like SEMrush or Ahrefs can help pinpoint issues such as broken links, slow page load speeds, or ineffective keyword targeting. These insights empower you to make informed adjustments before a major algorithm change occurs.

Equally important is ensuring that your content strategy remains adaptable. Experimenting with various content formats—like videos, infographics, and podcasts—and assessing their engagement levels can enhance your reach. A diverse content strategy caters to different audience preferences and mitigates risks associated with potential algorithm shifts that may favor certain media types over others. By creating comprehensive content that thoroughly addresses users' questions in an engaging manner, you reinforce your site's authority across multiple topics.

Investing in user experience (UX) enhancements is another critical aspect of SEO preparation. A website designed with intuitive navigation, mobile responsiveness, and fast load times not only resonates positively with users but also satisfies search engine criteria. Google's Core Web Vitals initiative emphasizes these factors; optimizing for them will help position you for success regardless of future algorithm changes. Prioritizing UX involves continuously analyzing user interactions through tools like Google Analytics or Hotjar to identify areas needing improvement.

Implementing a system for gathering real-time user feedback on your website's functionality and content relevance can provide invaluable insights. Platforms such as Qualaroo or UserTesting enable you to hear directly from users about their experiences. Understanding their needs not only enhances your offerings but also helps you proactively address any vulnerabilities that may arise during an algorithm update.

Building strong relationships with other industry professionals can also yield valuable intelligence on emerging trends or updates. Networking through SEO conferences or webinars fosters knowledge sharing that benefits all involved parties. Cultivating partnerships can lead to collaborative projects that enhance visibility and credibility—two factors that are especially crucial during uncertain times.

Finally, adopting a mindset of agility within your SEO strategy is essential. Regularly revisiting and revising your goals based on new information or shifts in the market landscape allows for rapid adjustments rather than long-term commitments that may become outdated following an algorithm update.

By actively preparing for the changes ahead, you position yourself as a leader in the industry instead of simply reacting when updates occur. This proactive approach not only secures your current standing but also sets the stage for future growth and innovation in the ever-evolving world of SEO.

EPILOGUE

The journey through the landscape of SEO in 2025 reveals the complexities and evolving strategies that define this essential discipline. By delving into everything from the fundamental principles of search engine functionality to the intricate relationship between user experience and algorithm changes, it becomes clear that mastering SEO requires a multifaceted approach. This endeavor extends beyond mere technical skills; it is a harmonious blend of creativity, strategy, and continual adaptation.

A central theme emerges from the insights gathered throughout this guide: staying ahead in SEO necessitates not just knowledge but also a steadfast commitment to innovation. The emergence of artificial intelligence and machine learning, for instance, has revolutionized our approach to keyword research and content optimization. By leveraging these technologies, SEO professionals can predict trends, customize user experiences, and significantly boost engagement metrics. Integrating AI tools like Clearscope or SurferSEO into your strategy will be crucial, enabling you to refine your content based on real-time data analytics.

The importance of high-quality content cannot be overstated. Creating valuable resources for users is essential; as many industry experts agree, informative and engaging content drives both organic traffic and conversions. To support this effort, developing an editorial calendar can streamline content creation while ensuring a diverse range of formats —such as articles, videos, and podcasts—that cater to varied audience preferences. Combining engaging storytelling with practical insights will help your brand stand out in crowded marketplaces.

Equally important is the critical role of backlinks. Building relationships within the industry and securing quality links should be ongoing priorities. Techniques like guest blogging and influencer outreach not only facilitate link acquisition but also enhance brand visibility. As you foster these connections, focus on cultivating genuine partnerships rather than pursuing transactional relationships.

Additionally, as local SEO gains prominence amidst increasing search personalization, businesses must invest in strategies that reflect this shift. Optimizing your Google My Business profile is vital for achieving local visibility. Encourage satisfied customers to leave reviews; their testimonials serve as social proof that can influence potential customers' decisions. Complementing these efforts with local keyword research ensures that your business appears in relevant searches.

Emphasizing continuous learning has been intentional throughout this guide—staying informed about industry shifts is key to proactive adaptation. Engaging with thought leaders on platforms like Twitter or participating in SEO-focused forums can keep you at the forefront of emerging best practices. Regularly conducting SEO audits will provide actionable insights to refine your strategy over time.

your journey as an SEO professional doesn't end here; it evolves as you embrace new challenges and opportunities within this dynamic field. As algorithms continue to change and user expectations shift, adaptability will become your greatest asset. Approach each day with curiosity and openness to experimentation; this mindset will empower you to explore new avenues while fine-tuning your existing strategies.

In summary, becoming an "SEO God" involves not only mastering current tactics but also anticipating future developments with foresight. Your ability to innovate and strategize will distinguish you from the competition as you navigate this ever-evolving digital landscape. The foundation laid in this book serves as a springboard into a future rich with potential, where you can actively shape search environments rather than merely reacting to them.

Your evolution begins now; take these lessons forward into your practice and watch how they transform your approach to achieving SEO success.

Recap of Key Strategies

This guide has explored a wide range of SEO strategies, revealing techniques and insights that are crucial for mastering search engine optimization. Now, let's distill these strategies into actionable takeaways that can enhance your efforts in 2025 and beyond.

Essentially of effective SEO is keyword research. It all begins with understanding user intent—recognizing why people search for specific terms and how their needs evolve over time. Tools like SEMrush and Ahrefs can help you identify high-traffic keywords while also uncovering long-tail opportunities that competitors might miss. This dual approach not only boosts visibility but also attracts targeted traffic that is more likely to convert.

Content creation is another foundational strategy. Producing high-quality, engaging content satisfies search algorithms and captivates users, fostering both retention and shares. Implementing an editorial calendar ensures consistency in your output and encourages diverse formats—from blog posts to videos—that cater to various audience preferences. Remember, weaving storytelling with practical insights can significantly enhance your brand's appeal, making your content both informative and memorable.

Building backlinks is essential for establishing authority and trustworthiness in your niche. The focus has shifted from quantity to quality; prioritizing genuine relationships through guest blogging or collaborations yields more sustainable results than chasing quick wins with questionable tactics. Each link should reflect your credibility, bolstering your site's overall standing in search results.

While often operating behind the scenes, technical SEO is equally critical for success. A well-structured website facilitates efficient crawling and indexing by search engines. Practices like optimizing site speed and ensuring mobile responsiveness greatly enhance user experience—a key ranking factor in today's digital landscape. Regular audits can help identify technical issues before they impact performance.

Local SEO has become increasingly important as businesses aim to capture hyperlocal markets. Optimizing your Google My Business profile is essential for visibility in local searches, complemented by soliciting reviews that build social proof. Conducting local keyword research further refines your strategy, aligning it with user expectations tied to geographical queries.

The integration of artificial intelligence into SEO strategies is another vital consideration. AI tools can streamline processes such as content optimization and keyword analysis, providing insights derived from real-time data analytics that inform decision-making. Staying abreast of AI advancements will empower you to effectively harness these innovations.

Lastly, cultivating a mindset of continuous learning and adaptation is crucial in a rapidly evolving digital landscape. Engaging with industry thought leaders on social media platforms or forums can offer valuable insights into emerging trends and best practices that keep you ahead of the curve. Regularly revisiting your strategies ensures they remain relevant amid changing algorithms and user behaviors.

By synthesizing these key strategies—keyword research based on user intent, compelling content creation, authoritative backlink building, robust technical foundations, localized optimizations, AI integration, and a commitment to lifelong learning—you equip yourself with the essential tools for success in the dynamic world of SEO. Each component interlocks with the others, creating a cohesive approach that positions you as an industry leader ready to embrace new challenges.

Embrace this knowledge not merely as information but as part of an ongoing journey toward excellence in SEO mastery. Your thoughtful implementation of these strategies will shape not only your success but also the future of digital marketing in an ever-changing landscape.

The Ever-Evolving Nature of SEO

The world of SEO is in a constant state of change, driven by technological advancements, evolving user behaviors, and the shifting algorithms of search engines. What worked effectively yesterday may not yield the same results tomorrow, making it essential for professionals in the field to adopt a mindset that embraces agility and foresight.

At the heart of this evolution is the recognition that user intent is paramount in search engine considerations. Simply optimizing for specific keywords is no longer enough; understanding the context behind those searches is crucial. Take this example, when users type "best hiking shoes" into a search engine, they could be looking for reviews, comparison articles, or even places to purchase them. Tools like Google Trends can provide insights into not just keyword popularity but also how interests shift over time, helping you grasp what your audience truly values. By aligning your content with these insights, you can create a more tailored experience that directly meets user needs.

In this dynamic landscape, content remains king, but its

form and delivery are constantly evolving. The rise of video content, podcasts, and interactive media has transformed the way information is consumed online. Platforms like TikTok and YouTube have redefined audience engagement strategies; short videos can convey information quickly and memorably—an advantage that traditional written content often struggles to match in terms of immediate impact. By embracing diverse formats and incorporating storytelling techniques into your content strategy, you can cater to varying preferences while ensuring continued relevance.

Complicating the SEO landscape further is the increasing integration of artificial intelligence and machine learning technologies into search algorithms. AI's capacity to analyze vast amounts of data enables search engines to deliver results that better align with user expectations. Understanding how these technologies function empowers SEO professionals to refine their strategies accordingly. For example, leveraging natural language processing tools can enhance keyword optimization efforts by identifying phrases that resonate with users' spoken queries—especially relevant as voice search continues to gain traction.

Equally important is staying informed about technical advancements in web design and development. A well-structured website architecture is fundamental for facilitating effective crawling and indexing by search engines. Regular technical audits can reveal issues such as broken links or slow load times that may hinder performance. Also, ensuring your site is mobile-friendly has become essential as mobile traffic continues to rise globally. With Google prioritizing mobile-first indexing, neglecting this aspect could severely impact your visibility.

As businesses increasingly target hyperlocal markets amid rising competition, local SEO tactics are becoming more pronounced. Claiming and optimizing your Google My Business listing with accurate information can significantly enhance visibility in local searches—a crucial step for brick-and-mortar establishments aiming to attract nearby customers. Additionally, encouraging customer reviews fosters social proof while boosting local rankings; positive feedback acts as a magnet for new clients.

Looking ahead, we must recognize the importance of continuous learning in this field. Engaging with industry experts through webinars or social media platforms provides fresh perspectives on emerging trends and keeps you updated on best practices that evolve over time. Regularly revising your strategies based on new insights will not only help maintain relevance but also position you as a thought leader within your niche.

SEO has transformed from a simple checklist into an intricate web of interconnected factors influenced by both technology and human behavior. By remaining vigilant to these shifts—embracing changes in user intent, content formats, algorithm updates, technical requirements, local dynamics, and educational opportunities—you ensure that your strategies remain innovative and effective.

As this landscape continues to evolve at an unprecedented pace, viewing these changes as opportunities rather than challenges will empower you to lead rather than follow in the realm of SEO excellence. Your proactive approach will significantly shape your journey through this complex field while contributing to its future dynamics along the way.

Encouragement for Continuous Learning

Continuous learning is essential in the ever-evolving field of SEO. The rapid changes in technology and user behavior require professionals to stay updated and actively seek knowledge beyond their current expertise. Take Sarah, for instance, a mid-level SEO specialist who initially concentrated on keyword optimization. As algorithm updates altered the landscape, she found herself frustrated. Instead of retreating, she decided to invest in her education by enrolling in online courses that explored emerging trends such as artificial intelligence and machine learning in SEO. This commitment transformed her perspective, enabling her to craft strategies that not only adhered to current standards but also positioned her ahead of the curve.

Engaging with industry thought leaders is another vital component of continuous growth. Social media platforms like Twitter and LinkedIn have become essential for following discussions about recent changes in search engine algorithms and effective content strategies. For example, participating in Twitter chats can provide real-time insights and innovative tactics shared by experts facing similar challenges. Joining SEO-focused groups on LinkedIn opens up networking opportunities and fosters the exchange of ideas, often igniting inspiration and revealing solutions you may not have considered.

Regularly reading industry publications is equally crucial for staying informed. Websites like Moz, Search Engine Journal, and Neil Patel's blog offer timely updates on search engine news, algorithm changes, and successful case studies. Engaging with these resources not only keeps you abreast of effective practices but also encourages experimentation with new approaches. By dedicating just an hour each week to this content, you can identify patterns and anticipate future shifts in the landscape.

Attending workshops and conferences can also serve as powerful catalysts for growth. Immersing yourself in an environment filled with like-minded professionals fosters collaboration and inspiration. At a recent SEO conference, for instance, attendees had the chance to interact directly with Google representatives discussing upcoming algorithm updates. Such insights are invaluable for adjusting strategies proactively rather than reactively. Additionally, these events often feature hands-on sessions where participants can learn new tools or techniques directly from experts—an experience that reinforces learning through practice.

Learning should extend beyond formal education or workshops; it's important to cultivate a mindset of curiosity and experimentation in your daily work. Each campaign presents an opportunity to test hypotheses, analyze outcomes, and refine strategies based on performance metrics. For example, if you launch a new piece of content optimized for voice search but don't see the anticipated engagement levels, dive into the analytics to better understand user behavior. Perhaps adjustments are needed for clarity or structure; recognizing these nuances fosters a culture of improvement driven by data rather than guesswork.

Feedback from peers is another valuable component of your continuous learning journey. Establishing a mentor-mentee relationship with someone more experienced can offer deeper insights into advanced strategies and common pitfalls. Conversely, sharing your knowledge with newcomers can solidify your understanding while providing fresh perspectives through their inquiries. This reciprocal relationship enriches both parties and nurtures an ongoing dialogue about best practices within the industry.

Finally, embracing failure as part of the learning process is critical. In SEO, not every tactic will yield immediate results; recognizing when something isn't working is just as important as celebrating successes. Conducting post-mortems on underperforming campaigns allows for honest reflection on what went wrong and why. This practice cultivates resilience and prepares you to pivot quickly—an essential skill in an industry defined by constant change.

As you navigate your professional path in SEO, make continuous learning a core value. Actively seek knowledge through various channels—whether online courses, industry publications, networking opportunities, or hands-on experiences—and cultivate an adaptable mindset that thrives amid change. Every step taken toward enhancing your skills not only reinforces your expertise but also positions you as a leader ready to embrace the future of search engine optimization with confidence and creativity.

Final Thoughts on Becoming an SEO God

Mastering SEO goes beyond merely understanding algorithms or adhering to best practices; it is a holistic journey that requires a blend of strategic thinking, creativity, and an unwavering commitment to growth. To become an SEO expert —often referred to as an "SEO God"—is to transcend the typical boundaries of digital marketing. It involves fostering an innovative mindset that embraces the ever-evolving landscape of search engine optimization.

Consider the journeys of top professionals in the industry, those who have reached the pinnacle of SEO expertise. They did not arrive at this level by resting on their achievements. Instead, they consistently pushed boundaries, experimented with new technologies, and learned from both their successes and failures. A notable example is Rand Fishkin, co-founder of Moz and SparkToro, whose relentless pursuit of knowledge and willingness to share insights has propelled not only his career but also the entire industry forward.

To truly excel in SEO, start with a deep understanding of your audience. This involves looking beyond demographics to explore psychographics—what motivates them, what challenges they face, and how they engage with content online. Gaining this insight enables you to create tailored experiences that resonate deeply with users, driving both engagement and conversions. When you have a genuine grasp of your audience's needs, crafting compelling content becomes second nature.

Analytics play a crucial role in this process. By effectively leveraging tools like Google Analytics or SEMrush, you can uncover valuable insights into user behavior and site performance. Take this example, if you notice users dropping off at a specific point in your sales funnel, take a closer look at the content in that area. It may lack clarity or fail to address key concerns; making adjustments could significantly enhance user retention and satisfaction.

Building strong relationships within the industry is equally vital. Networking is not just about attending events; it's about cultivating genuine connections with peers and mentors who can challenge your thinking and offer fresh perspectives. Engaging with communities on platforms like Reddit or specialized SEO forums can lead to meaningful discussions that spark new ideas. Remember that collaboration often produces more innovative solutions than working alone.

In addition to networking, embrace experimentation as part of your strategy development process. Test various approaches— whether it's different content formats or diverse optimization tactics—and analyze which yield the best results for your unique context. For example, A/B testing landing pages can reveal what resonates most with your audience; even small changes in headlines or call-to-action placements can lead to significant improvements in conversion rates.

Cultivating resilience in the face of setbacks is equally essential. In an environment where algorithm changes can disrupt established strategies overnight, maintaining a positive outlook is crucial for long-term success. Rather than fearing failure, learn from each misstep; every unsuccessful campaign provides lessons that refine future efforts.

Innovation should remain at the forefront of your approach as well. As we look toward 2025 and beyond, emerging technologies like artificial intelligence will continue to reshape search engine dynamics profoundly. By adopting tools that integrate AI-driven insights into your strategies, you'll not only stay competitive but also streamline workflows.

Lastly, maintain an insatiable curiosity about all facets of SEO —from technical nuances to broader trends affecting the global digital marketing landscape. Subscribe to leading industry publications and podcasts for insights into new developments; this commitment will ensure you remain informed about shifts before they become mainstream.

In summary, becoming an SEO God is less about achieving a specific title and more about embodying a mindset dedicated to continuous improvement and innovation in search engine optimization practices. Fully commit to understanding user needs, leveraging analytics for actionable insights, networking within the community for diverse perspectives, experimenting boldly with strategies, nurturing resilience through failures, and creatively leveraging emerging technologies—all these elements converge into a powerful approach toward mastering SEO.

As you continue on this journey toward excellence in search engine optimization, remember: true mastery lies not just in knowledge but in action. Consistent action fueled by learning and adaptation will ultimately define your success as an SEO leader in 2025 and beyond.

www.ingramcontent.com/pod-product-compliance
Lightning Source LLC
LaVergne TN
LVHW051223050326
832903LV00028B/2236